MW01178264

THE
TRANSFORMATIONAL
ORGANIZATION
PARADIGM

**Thriving in Greyscale and Producing Results
Through Continuous Transformation**

By Dr. Linda L. Miller

ISBN-13: 978-1512215045

ISBN-10: 151221504X

Publisher : iMind Transformation, A Division of Syncopa Management Inc. Vancouver, British Columbia

www.imindtransformation.com

With special acknowledgement to:

The Harvard Business Review 1993, 1995

and

The Harvard Business Review on Change 1998

Contents |

Preface |

"In the past decade, the author has watched more than 100 companies try to remake themselves into better competitors. Their efforts have gone under many banners: total quality management, reengineering, right sizing, restructuring, cultural change, and turnarounds. In almost every case, the goal has been the same: to cope with a new, more challenging market by changing how business is conducted.

A few of those efforts have been very successful. A few have been utter failures. Most fall somewhere in between, with a distinct tilt toward the lower end of the scale. The lessons that can be learned will be relevant to more and more organizations as the business environment becomes increasingly competitive in the coming decade.

One lesson is that change involves numerous phases that, together, usually take a long time. Skipping steps creates only an illusion of speed and never produces a satisfying result. A second lesson is that critical mistakes in any of the phases can have a devastating impact, slowing momentum and negating previous gains."

- John P. Kotter, Harvard Business Review on Change 1998

Business professionals and the world at large have seen a 'New Millennium' shift in how business is conducted emerge over the past 30 years, and so far, organizations who have attempted to transform to meet the new demands of this new 'age' have made less progress and spent more money than they ever imagined.

Through that time, and regardless of the angle of approach: financial meltdown, globalization, competitive re-positioning, consumer demand, or talent retention - <u>continuous</u> transformation has become the new reality... a reality with properties so different than what we have known, that a good deal of unlearning of the ways in which business is conducted has to be done before significant forward movement is possible.

This combination of circumstances represents an entirely new paradigm for organization structure, and ways of working that will continue to emerge over the next 30 years.

This book refers to this phenomenon as the *Transformational Organization Paradigm* and takes the position that moving from their current paradigm into a transformational paradigm is not optional for most companies in the post-millennial world.

The Transformational Organization Paradigm is a method and a style; it is a philosophy and a strategy; it is a tool *and* an outcome; it is a way of being. It is a set of shifts that are applied to shape the organization to match the accelerated pace of business, and that evolves leadership capability and the tenor in which communication with employees and business partners takes place.

Under the Transformational Organization Paradigm, levers for motivating change and agility that are already present in the organization become more prominent, have a pervasive presence in day to day work, and create lift and leverage in new ways. The outcomes of applying the methods, practices and tools associated with the Transformational Organization Paradigm are measurable, tangible, and evidence-based.

THIS BOOK

This book talks about transformation as a permanent state of operation for the organization. It accepts and proposes that the interpretation of the *optimal transformational paradigm* for each organization is different based on the particular nature of the enterprise.

The ideas in this book are expressed in terms of the kinds of activities, habits, and capabilities that an organization must shift toward in order travel at a *transformative* level and move in transformation ways. This book answers in broad terms the questions "What is it?", "What does it look like" and "What are we aiming for?" when it comes to describing the new transformational paradigm that is becoming our day to day reality. And also discusses 'why' the new paradigm has come into being in practical terms.

In most sections the Transformational Organization Paradigm is described in terms of the kind and nature of communication that is occurring, and the kind and nature of the leadership that is occurring. Altering these two foundational aspects of day to day business is a big part of the work in developing a transformational paradigm within an organization. Where possible, examples and metaphors are used to convey ideas and bring home the tone and tenor of the ideas in the material.

Research for this book was conducted over an 8 year period from 2004 to 2015 and encompassed observations and conversations with clients as well as a review of scholarly and popular written works by professionals in psychology, human resources, business management, leadership, and information technology.

The information in this book is supported by a formal framework and methodology titled *"The Continuous Transformation Framework and Method"* which lays out the "how" portion of achieving the Transformational Organization Paradigm in appropriate, meaningful and deliberate shifts.

AUTHOR SYNOPSIS

As a business and Information Technology professional, I have observed the approaching, and now surrounding transformative events which shape the New Millennium business environment. And although I have been a practitioner of, culture/values shift, business change management, restructuring, outsourcing, and transformative technology application, none of these disciplines can approach the magnitude of change that faces pre-millennium organizations who are trying to gear up to New Millennium demands.

With the world converging on wholesale electronification of the average person's life, and industrial-age methods starting to do more harm than good for the bottom line, I thought the time was right to introduce practical transformational adaptation techniques as a corporate capability – a capability every organization should consider an absolute must for survival and positioning for future prosperity.

FOUNDATIONAL THEORIES

A portion of the inspiration for this book is found in the theories and practices below:

- Transformational Leadership and Transactional Leadership as defined by James MacGregor Burns and Bernard M. Bass
- Participatory Organization as defined by Tim O'Reilly
- Motivational Interviewing as defined by William R. Miller and Stephen Rollnick
- Emotional Intelligence as defined by Daniel Goleman
- Social Intelligence as defined by Ross Honeywill
- Change Immunity as defined by Robert Kegan and Lisa Laskow Lahey
- Group Genius as defined by Matt Taylor and Gail Taylor
- Communication Loop as defined by Westley and MacLean
- Ingenuity Pathways as defined by Jimenez-Marin and M Collado Romero
- Innovation as defined by Peter F. Drucker
- Disruptive Innovation Theory as defined by Clayton M. Christensen and Joseph Bower
- Complex Adaptive Systems and Chaos Theory as defined by N.K. Hayles and I. Prigogine and D. Colander
- Theory X and Y as defined by Douglas McGregor
- Flux and Transformation Metaphor as defined by Gareth Morgan

The Transformational Organization |

A misalignment between pre-millennial organizations (i.e., those organizations that were created prior to the great transformation that we are living through) and post-millennial customer demands has been emerging for the last 30 years. In the last 5 years a balance point has been tipped in the method by which most businesses are organized and managed. Organizations that have resisted or avoided genuine transformation are at risk of being consumed by ones that are able to survive and thrive in the post-Millennial world.

The New Millennium arrived with a big bang of transformative events for many organizations...

- Customers demanding a more intimate relationship with service providers
- Employees demanding a more meaningful relationship with employers
- Downward pressure on funding produces a greater reliance on automation as leverage
- Radical alteration of internal business systems for intelligence flow
- Radical alteration of internal business functions for lean and agile delivery
- Lean and agile competitors driving a repositioning within the marketplace

There is a cyclical pattern here that we can expect to continue into the latter half of the 21st century, at an ever escalating speed. Perpetuated on one side by a congealing and solidification of consumer intelligence and demand-enablement through economic pressure and social media expression, and perpetuated on the other side by, distillation and crystallization of worker wisdom empowerment as a result of transference of responsibility through downsizing , increased accessibility to 'worldly' knowledge, and development of multiple specialization expertise.

In order to come into sync with the "New Millennium" way of doing business, a shift in how leadership is conducted and how employees regard change is necessary. Forward motion at all costs is the order of the day, however the employees of the company are mired in ill-fitting and partially complete alterations to their environment. Best intentions about applying change management practices have met with insufficient pull-through of changes into full competence and capability toward the strategic vision. Quite simply the effort applied, while enormous in many cases, has missed the point - being neither incisive enough, nor participative enough to enable the magnitude of adaptation required. And the effects of this have been literally disabling for many organizations - while the clock is ticking.

Beyond that, in order to free up the kind of dynamic energy required to achieve greater speed and agility in responding to transformative demands/events, traditional ways of setting goals, developing people, and motivating people have to change. In other words, executing transformative initiatives based on strategy and providing support and education about change management is not enough. Becoming a transformational organization is a whole-enterprise and permanent shift in the approach to and methods by which business is conducted and in how the organizations' people think, lead, manage, and relate.

An appropriate way to describe what we have come to know as organizational transformation is that it is an *adaptive response* to a *transformative event* that has already occurred. Following a transformational method presents a way to put the adaptive response into action, a way to understand the meaning of the transformative event and direct and redirect organizational resources to successfully adapt as the events unfurl their implications. From another perspective, adopting transformational methods provides the organization with discrete, evidence-based ways of matching the 'pulse' or 'frequency' of the transformative event and formulating a corresponding scale and rhythm of adaptation in accordance with the scale of the transformative event. The goal is to tune adaptive activities to the same 'wavelength' as the transformative event they are addressing and move with and through each successive transformation in lock-step-leap-frog fashion.

With the speed of change having increased so dramatically the pattern of continuous transformation has become visible and predictable. Still, transformation cannot be imposed, and it is much more than a one-off exercise in culture shift. Transformation transcends classic change management techniques and tactics, and overarches enterprise toolsets and architectures. However, traditional business change practices are still applied (and now need to be applied) at all levels by specialists and by leaders and managers. The characteristics of what it is to be a transformational organization are very clear.

The necessary concepts and abilities to successfully transform on an ongoing basis can be taught and in fact without such knowledge and skills executives, leaders, and workers cannot receive and actuate *any* transformation. The sooner an organization realistically confronts what it must alter to become its own version of a continuously transformational organization, and then begins cyclical transformations using a prescribed set of methods and practices, the better off its people, its consumers, and its bottom line will be.

THE CHALLENGE OF THE NEW-MILLENIUM BUSINESS ENVIRONMENT

A formal definition of the term New Millennium 'Age' could not be located and so the following is offered for the purposes of this book:

New Millennium Business is characterised by a humanistic approach in how business adapts to new and greater consumer intelligence and power, the raising of marketplace minimum entry requirements for technology connectedness, and the necessity for compression of complex systems and processes into simple accessibility.

Achievement demands: a re-balancing of the development of the technical aspects and social aspects to achieve optimum internal collaboration and adaptive response; a consideration of the organization as a system of interacting, mutually dependent parts; and a reliance on synchronous co-creation among and between those parts.

Moving forward at all costs along relationships that are genuinely based in intrinsic motivation and intrinsic wisdom, where work is conducted under transformational leadership and participative management to realize business objectives is the norm.

Whew!

That said, it is the opinion of this book that we do not know what this next 'Age' is all about. We can only take steps to transform in the general direction indicated above and from that new vantage point, discern the next emerging context.

The effect that downsizing and matrix management have had on how people interact over the past 3 decades has become an embittering and disempowering part of our corporate landscape. We knew what we were doing at the time – preparing for a more dynamic way of doing business, moving from Industrial Age command and control methods to information age participative and innovative methods. And we knew we would have to straddle both worlds for a few years - these were a half-steps toward what we are now facing as we move into the next stage of a 60-year transformation to meaning-driven, value-network and group-genius environments.

This next part of the transformative journey makes adaptation and innovation a worker responsibility. It asks the management and staff that are straddling the hierarchical and cross-functional models to lift both feet and hover in the space of their own expertise while interacting in constant connectedness with others who have functional touch-points to their work.

Management under this 'co-creation' scenario becomes more about channeling effort and thought toward business goals and outcomes. Leadership becomes a distinctly separate activity from management and is conducted by all people at all levels. And leadership has more to do with inspiring others to see potential and realizing when new states of operation are achieved beyond the metrics that management is managing to. Decisions are made by every individual within the role they play at any given time, fuelled by strengths-based collaboration and aimed at realizing the characteristics of the business transformation objectives within the window of opportunity available.

A jumping off point for this next part of the transformative journey is the time we have spent looking back over projects and decisions that were taken debriefing, decomposing, and digesting what happened. This effort has served as a cradle for developing some innate wisdom about the balance points of risk, the trade-offs that the pressure to deliver (coercion) presents, the timing and placement of the use of intuition, the inevitability of reciprocity during the expenditure of great volumes of effort to change, and of the effects of lacking leadership commitment in the face of stretched resources.

Now that most everyone has a feel for this new reality consciously or unconsciously, it's easier acknowledge the ambiguity and paradoxes that transformation presents. From now on, though, effort spent looking back only serves to hold us there as the New Millennium marches onward.

Another factor in working through the next phase of the transformative journey is that the addiction to command and control built up over (arguably) the last 5000 years is proving to be more deeply ingrained than we thought – change is perceived as punitive in nature under Industrial Age thinking and amidst the overwhelm of ambiguous reporting structures and missing links between authority and accountability, and responsibility and ownership. Workplace stress levels reach new heights annually across all levels of the organization due to the dissonance between where the world is heading and what methods are in use in the workplace.

How do we call a halt to the churn that this creates? How do we see and move past the matrix organization half-way point that many seem to be stuck at? What expectations can we set about what the next stage in becoming fully transformational will demand of us? How do we address the fears about lack of control in the New Millennium?

The answer to these questions is as much about an absence of action as trying to build anything in particular. That is, moving into a Transformational Organization Paradigm for doing business as the New Millennium demands is as much about supporting a letting go the remainder of Industrial Age command and control methods, as it is about developing new ways of thinking, creating, and operating.

To put this in terms of commonly understood change psychology, a decade into the New Millennium and 50 years into the Information Age, we are finally moving out of the denial, anger and bargaining stages of Kublar's *5 Stages of Grief and Loss*, where letting go of beloved hierarchical Industrial Age command and control methods are concerned. And we are moving out of the bargaining and depression stages where our acceptance of the scale and breadth of the adaptation to the New Millennium 'Age' is concerned. Here is a diagram of Kublars 5 Stages of Greif and Loss:

Think of the above as *states* rather than stages when applying them to organizational and business change. Individuals, groups and teams will move in and out of these states quickly or slowly as well as the organization as a whole moving in and out of these states quickly or slowly.

While we could argue whether one state applies more readily to the business transformation experience than another, the point here is that our boards and executive and our managers and staff are realizing that in order to transform they can't go on thinking and behaving anything like they always have and a concerted effort at all levels is required to bring a shift in thinking about *before* transformation can occur.

In other words, this is not about tuning management practices, or harnessing the power of information technology, or engaging stakeholders and staff – it's about getting serious about matching how we originate, orient, and conduct business with the nature and characteristics of the New Millennium. To do this we must unlearn what we have learned that has made us successful individually and corporately.

Organizations and the people within them are shifting in and out of the denial, anger, bargaining, and depression states when wrestling with the foreign-ness of what the New Millennium business world is demanding. They are practicing a fair amount of avoidance to 'going all the way there' as they execute transformational initiatives in versions of the same old way they executed strategic growth initiatives.

While all this goes on, a simple truth surfaces in glimpses : Transformation has nothing to do with grief and loss at all, it has to do with opportunity and evolution. And it's comprised of painful, stretching, shattering shifts in thinking and behaving that are required to achieve the New Millennium mindset. Once learned, transformational methods that are inherent in New Millennium business become reality as we know it.

NEW MILLENNIUM CONSUMER POWER

> *In 2015, the 'millennials' generation will*
> *grow to a population greater than the 'boomers'.*

> -Numerous Articles

As social media matures with the Millennium demographic, it forms the basis of consumer demand power that goes beyond 'on-demand' to 'predictive' - to the extent that meeting consumer demand can be expected to become a speculative activity. Short term demand yields cash flow and profits now and magnetizes a market anticipation compass showing where the next demand might come from. And, although this might seem to be more aligned with the departing 'disposable' society than we are comfortable with, the social connectedness mindset is combined with a new flavor of austerity that is based in the green movement as well as a departure from the greedy consumerism of the past century.

Doing more day to day and doing more with less translates to a more mindful, more discerning, and more appreciative and loyal customer base for most companies. Consumers are expecting a good deal for free from their supplier companies in exchange for an open mind and a slice of attention large enough to win business.

What consumers are and are not buying and what they are expecting their suppliers to DO, and what they are expecting their suppliers NOT to do will be public knowledge day to day, etched into the permanent knowledgebase of humanity for all time.

With a half-dozen conversations going at the same time on a variety of mediums and channels, the New Millennium consumer and can't slow

8

down to follow corporate processes and procedures. They have less and less tolerance for lengthy processes and cumbersome interfaces – rejecting the workload that their supplier pushes on them for the privilege of purchasing a product or paying government fees. This workload comes back to the organization in greater volumes of 'exception handling' that cut into profits in the face of growing pressures to keep prices low. Until, that is, corporate systems and functions are adapted to accommodate this new way of thinking.

As the consumer raises to a position of greater leverage and influence at work and in the marketplace, they in turn must leave behind the more mundane aspects of administering their lives. And here is where both corporations and individuals have common interest. For as the consumer spends less time commuting to work, the corporation must fund less office space. And as the consumer seeks to spend less time on household chores in favor of pursuing good health and having fulfilling life and work experiences in which they contribute more and more of themselves to the world at large, the corporation benefits from greater productivity, ingenuity and investment of energy.

This expresses the new face of consumer and employee 'loyalty' in the New Millennium. A distinctly old-fashioned yet ultra-modern interpretation of what it is to be a productive member of society. A whole lot less car washing and lawn mowing, and a whole lot more excursion and expression out into the world, meeting new people and exchanging ideas.

A common argument is that trying to connect to others in great volumes online cannot possibly have more meaning than keeping a home. The point is that this is the glaring truth of the New Millennium world. Connectedness learning takes place by absorbing the thoughts and trends of thought of a great number of people having different perspectives with great speed to come to a decision or take a forward-moving action that also yields greater support and certainty and occurs at the most opportune time. In short, New Millennium connectedness is all about being in the right place at the right time. And *this* is something both organizations and their consumers find great value in – it is *leverage*, and it is the fertile ground of the New Millennium economy.

To put a fine point on it, without the distraction of consuming for the sake of consuming, and with increasing health and vitality, the average consumer is free to apply their abilities more fully to that common ground where their interests overlap with the interests of their suppliers and their employer. The power of the consumer and the power of the employee is based in inter-connectedness in the New Millennium world.

MORE THAN BEHAVIOUR CHANGE – INTEGRATION OF INFORMATION TECHNOLOGY AND ORGANIZATIONAL DEVELOPMENT

So transformation, then, begins at the resignation stage of Kublar's *5 Stages of Grief and Loss*, and moves toward acceptance, and ultimately commitment of ones-self to the transformative tasks at hand. With this in mind a different change-related model that also supports modern Change Management methods enters the picture - the Transtheoretical Model (Prochaska) of Behaviour Change.

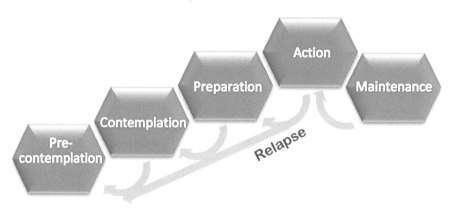

In the Transtheoretical Model, change is a process involving progressing through a series of stages, where, again, the individual, group or team may move back and forth between stages. However this model is much more linear and primarily about *doing* rather than *feeling* as compared with the previous model. Here are the WIKI definitions of the Transtheoretical Model stages of change:

1. Pre-contemplation (Not Ready) -"People are not intending to take action in the foreseeable future, and can be unaware that their behaviour is problematic"
2. Contemplation (Getting Ready)-"People are beginning to recognize that their behaviour is problematic, and start to look at the pros and cons of their continued actions"
3. Preparation (Ready) -"People are intending to take action in the immediate future, and may begin taking small steps toward behaviour change"
4. Action – "People have made specific overt modifications in modifying their problem behaviour or in acquiring new healthy behaviours"
5. Maintenance – "People have been able to sustain action for a while and are working to prevent relapse"
6. Termination – "Individuals have zero temptation and they are sure they will not return to their old unhealthy habit as a way of coping"
7. In addition, the researchers conceptualized "relapse" (recycling) which is not a stage in itself but rather the "return from Action or Maintenance to an earlier stage."

This model has been referenced in support of the change-plateau-change lifecycle that is commonly applied when talking about business evolution and growth. With the New Millennium speed, scale and constancy of change exploding the notion of 'plateau' this model might best be applied to that which it was originally designed: the breaking of addiction.

In awaking to the realization that Industrial Age thinking and methods are so entrenched as to rival an 'addictive' construct, applying a corresponding set of psychological tools, adapted for business, is a reasonable approach.

In the opinion of this book, the transformation dialogue occurs outside of the 5 stages of grief and loss and the 5 stages of change models. In order for transformation to occur a wholesale leap beyond grief or loss associated with change is required in order to get it to happen. For the purposes of describing the Transformational Organization Paradigm this book will refer to this leap as 'Leap of Faith'.

And, in order for transformation to happen, pre-contemplation and contemplation stages are compressed with a foreshortened preparation stage.

What *is* relevant about the two models, where transformation is concerned, is that they both relate to the significant changes in thinking, behaviour and practice that must take place within organizational design and development, human motivation and leadership, and management and administration to achieve the Transformational Organization Paradigm as a successful and a continuous 'norm'. Without making this shift, your organization cannot meet the demands of the New Millennium.

Still, organizations are attempting to adapt to transformative events by reengineering, reinventing, restructuring and rethinking their strategies, structures, and expertise - typically around web-based, information rich, collaboration oriented, technology. These efforts have produced a type of 'digital Darwinism' for the Board and the Executive to approximate their progress and relative achievement of transformation into a New Millennium-savvy business. However, the stretching effect of downsizing and flattening has left large gaps between the executive and management and management and staff. And, regardless of the masses and masses of data IT has been pouring in to fill these gaps, they remain and are having a debilitating effect. Along the road to accomplish transformation, we as business leaders and we as IT leaders neglected to adequately govern the one asset that must be sound and stable going into the New Millennium world... Data.

Whether by accident, negligence, or design, corporate data is a mess. In fact, it is the opinion of this book that corporate data can never be anything but a mess unless and until the way in which business is conducted fully seats itself in the Information Age, and has rooted out Industrial Age thinking and methods. It is impossible to mobilize data so that it may be converted to information, translated into knowledge then integrated to produce corporate wisdom when the founding thought-base is geared toward: separation of people from knowledge; punishment/reward motivation around access to information; competitive systems that promote exclusion from knowledge; and command and

12

control of how information is consumed – the hallmarks of Industrial Age methods.

Addressing the 'data and information' portion of the transformation equation is a safe, detached way of starting in on the transformational journey. However once begun, work to transmute data into information, information into knowledge, and knowledge into wisdom must occur in leap-frog fashion *with* the human behavior, organizational behaviour, and organizational structure aspects of transformation that pave the way for this to occur.

For the past three decades business experts have been talking about the Information Age, and it appears that this 'age' is already passing from view. The so-called Information Age was/is a stepping stone into whatever the New Millennium 'Age' becomes. So far this 'age' is characterised by self-efficacy, entitlement, sharing, acceptance, and interconnectedness.

A commonly drawn diagram to explain the fundamental shifts required to transform from an Industrial Age, Hierarchical organization to an Information Age, Participative organization has been adapted slightly for the purposes of this book:

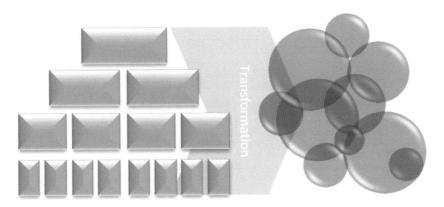

Formalized and Separated Interpersonal Relationships
Rigid Procedures and Communication Channels
Anonymity in the Face of Challenges
Command and Control Change Implementation
Strict Hierarchical Decision Making
Little Real Collaboration

Dynamic and Interconnected Interpersonal Relationships
Flexible, Technology and Knowledge-Enabled Framework
Role-Based Leadership and Individual Accountability for Change
Synchronous Communication and Shared Change Stewardship
Navigate a Sea of Unknowns With Ingenuity and Innovation
Participative Decision Making

Even visually, there is a sense of a completely different way of thinking and relating between people which exceeds the commonly understood Information Age definition. Regardless, underlying the transformative shifts are organizational design, organizational behaviour and positive psychology theories, modalities, and methods. The Transformational Organization Paradigm extracts elements from the following theories, modalities and methods as its foundation for transmuting corporations fully into the Information Age and orients them toward the emerging 'age':

- Transformational Leadership and Transactional Leadership as defined by James MacGregor Burns and Bernard M. Bass
- Participatory Organization as defined by Tim O'Reilly
- Motivational Interviewing as defined by William R. Miller and Stephen Rollnick
- Emotional Intelligence as defined by Daniel Goleman
- Social Intelligence as defined by Ross Honeywill
- Change Immunity as defined by Robert Kegan and Lisa Laskow Lahey
- Group Genius as defined by Matt Taylor and Gail Taylor
- Communication Loop as defined by Westley and MacLean
- Ingenuity Pathways as defined by Jimenez-Marin and M Collado Romero
- Innovation as defined by Peter F. Drucker
- Disruptive Innovation Theory as defined by Clayton M. Christensen and Joseph Bower
- Complex Adaptive Systems and Chaos Theory as defined by N.K. Hayles and I. Prigogine and D. Colander
- Theory X and Y as defined by Douglas McGregor
- Flux and Transformation Metaphor as defined by Gareth Morgan

Thankfully, these theories and their associated modalities and techniques have been employed in various behavioural and psychological applications for more than 30 years. Business can adapt and reinvent a good deal from these bodies of work as it seeks ways to cultivate the behavioural change befitting realization of Information Age and Millennium Age leadership, governance and management methods, and more importantly as a toolkit for addressing the people-side of transformation.

This book offers a practical distillation of the theories, modalities, and methods mentioned above into a discrete set of definitions, methods and practices for companies to seat themselves fully in Information Age methods and shed persistent Industrial Age habits, while developing continuous transformation capability. Taken together these three activities summarize the journey toward achievement of the Transformational Organization Paradigm.

Recognizing that not all organizations are or should be transforming at the same pace or on the same scale it is safe to say that forward motion at all costs is paramount. In fact not adapting quickly enough rivals financial control as the primary business risk of the 21st century. However backlogged change is crippling the ability of the organization to achieve the necessary speed and responsiveness required to adapt and survive. Indeed employees are mired in ill-fitting and partially complete alterations to their environment and are adrift in the low-management and low-leadership space between Industrial Age methods and Information Age methods. Best intentions about applying change management practices have yielded insufficient pull-through of changes toward the transformative vision of the new agile corporation in most cases.

And so, dealing with the backlog of change such that employees are receiving and adapting to more and more transformative change under an oppressive track record of incomplete change is one of the purposes that the methods and practices associated with the Transformational Organization Paradigm fulfill. Furthermore the injection of the methods and practices prepare staff for the new leadership and management methods that accompany the wholesale shift to continuous transformation.

Chapter References:

5 stages of change described by psychologist James O. Prochaska 1977

5 stages of grief and loss by psychologist Elisabeth Kubler-Ross 1969

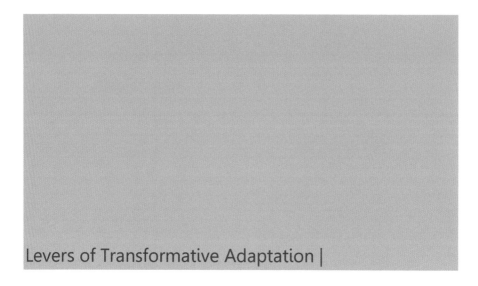

Levers of Transformative Adaptation |

When professionals talk about the differences between pre-millennium organizational structures and post-millennial organizational structures they instinctively draw a series of squares for the former and a series of circles for the latter. Currently most organizations are straddling both, routinely trying to make a square peg fit into a round hole.

Past formulas for success have opposite effects and surfing from transformation to transformation requires a different manner of organizational thinking. Latitudes of engagement among and between executive and management, and management and staff previously disallowed must be ignited and given leave. Maintaining fiscally responsible governance under this context requires a corresponding shift.

Transformational methods pivot on the people aspect of transformative change in terms of instilling and inspiring leadership and motivating people toward their optimal contribution under the New Millennium organization, which operates on an integrated foundation of good business principles and best information technology practices aimed at synchronizing adaptation efforts to transformative events.

Technology has been both a culprit and a resource in transformation that have been unfolding. As customers and employees demand more in shorter timeframes because of the availability of personal technology

16

tools and a broader understanding of process, more technology can be strategically applied by the organization in turn to support their people and processes in meeting those demands. Provided that the human behavior and organizational behavior portions of the transformation equation are addressed, the net effect of information technology on the imperative to transform should naturally balance out.

Change Management experts say that the best way to mitigate resistance to change is not to incur it in the first place. And the methods in this book come at the matter of transformational change first through the elimination of organizational friction, and second through reduction of cognitive dissonance (the feeling of discomfort when simultaneously holding two or more conflicting ideas, beliefs, values or emotional reactions). Business transformation is something that occurs at an individual level within the minds of its employees. Each individual must make a decision about participating in the overwhelming changes to some degree and a critical mass of individual participation is needed for transformative change to take hold and 'turn the ship'. This is nothing new.

The paradigm described in this book was defined to meet the approaching readiness in organizations for an evolved way of communicating and producing work that is based in an interconnected value-mindset, and an unarticulated desire on-balance to be in the transformed state already. And, while the work of shifting to a Transformational Organization Paradigm appears huge, the work to do to instill it is not as huge an undertaking as it might sound because of this growing readiness. To be successful, the work does require a distinct and permanent shift in appetite within the organization for continuous adaptation, 'newness', and the adventure of the unknown. In other words, the staff of the organization will need to find new comfort levels with ambiguity, complexity, and autonomy.

The Transformational Organization Paradigm is a permanent state and not a transitory gearing up for change then plateauing onto a new normal. Transformative thinking is present at all times and this is _the_ primary outcome of doing the work to become a transformational organization.

Transformational organizations make change management a staple skillset and competency at all levels of the organization. The way of thinking under a transformative model is productive through different means than the predominant hierarchical command and control and matrix managed models. Taken to the extreme transformational organizations foster new thought in their people and applaud individual movement and expression of any kind, using this as the primary resource for continued viability and health *rather than* money.

Going beyond the knowledge worker, as we have coined the term, the extreme transformational organization assumes first and foremost that it has no workers that are not knowledge workers regardless of whether workers are supported by adequate information technology or not. The transformational organization has no workers that are not also leaders. And the work its people conduct so clearly applies to the business strategic goals that the time spent on talking about whether or not there is alignment to strategic goals shifts entirely to focussing on re-interpreting strategic goals according to the knowns that have surfaced since their inception.

Other New Millennium business methods focus on a single instance of a transformation, and use terminology like unfreeze, change, refreeze. While they seem more palatable and *normal*, these methods don't address the longer term aspects of enabling, leading and managing ceaseless transformative change. The methods described in this book provide a lasting shift in thinking where change is concerned and open up lasting channels for change to flow into and through the minds of the people who make transformation realization possible.

In the transformatively agile corporation everything must be in flux at all times. This generates the momentum and fluidity required to adapt in sync with emergent market demands and new transformative events within and outside of the business environment. To consider that some aspect of work processes and tools can be locked down is a recipe for failure.

While other paradigms focus on 'ownership' and 'justification' the Transformational Organization Paradigm focusses on eliciting forward motion through 'pulling' techniques rather than 'pushing' techniques. Buy-in and reward are eliminated when individuals and teams can readily see that their contribution is valued and produces positive outcomes. An emphasis of a showing rather than telling is present that is not about evangelizing some distant ideal, but rather enabling individual decisions day to day in an organization that is shifting and changing radically day to day. A focus on enabling the asking and answering of hard questions emphasizes two-way communication with context-appropriate and reciprocal feedback mechanisms. The transformational organization shifts from 'authenticity' of interpersonal communication to 'genuine-ness' of connection with others.

Transformational organization approaches are intended to precede, focus and also work along-side classic change management, reaching into the context of the individual and team to generate a pulling effect for transformative work on a team, project, and enterprise level. The approaches focus on equipping staff with skills, capabilities and non-technology mechanisms geared for day to day under continuous transformative change.

SQUARE PEG – ROUND HOLE

In the spirit of square pegs and round holes, initial transformative efforts require us to navigate the maze in order to build the community of dynamically interconnecting spheres.

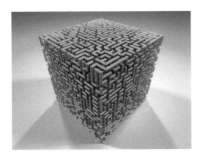 

We are asking people to navigate this…   to get to this…

When most organizations embark upon transformative change, they miss and important fact that what they are asking their people to do is : Navigate an uncharted multi-dimensional maze where communication and throughput is channelled along ridged but obscure pathways, defined by ever-increasing volumes of policy, regulation and process to create a polar opposite structure where functional units are formed and disbanded or jump from one *sphere* of functional work to another as needed, where spheres are held together by a common understanding of what is required to be a successful enterprise, and units define and execute their optimal function, as work products are consumed by spheres moving along or intersecting an orbital pathway of another sphere.

It is plain that we are asking the impossible here and that even the smallest work to transform is monumental under this circumstance. So the Transformational Organization Paradigm steps back and asks how transformation might occur without the drag placed on it by pre-millennium paradigms.

A number of organizational development experts suggest enveloping the business functions about to undergo transformative work in a bubble of free-flowing innovation and co-creation, matching as much as possible the target culture and organization design of the transformed state. That is, lifting off the old organization model completely so that the transformation can be constructed successfully.

The Transformational Organization Paradigm and associated methods and practices complement and enable this approach but don't' recommend it because of the strain caused when the transformed function begins to relate to functions still working under the old paradigm. Good work is quashed as soon as it encounters the non-adapted business functions that are not prepared nor aligned to receive it. The square pegs and round holes among leaders and managers and workers are abundantly apparent, cripple communication between groups, and threaten the success of the transformed function in a way that can irrevocably damage the viability of future transformative work. The Transformational Organization Paradigm offers levers that can be applied to lift off enough of the burden of the old paradigm across the enterprise to allow sufficient space for transformative adaptation to get traction and find a safer path to success.

THE LEVERS

Transformational Organization Paradigm methods are about mobilizing and remobilizing people and their inner resources that they may apply to their work life that are currently untapped. This mobilization is not a crisis response. It consists of a constant preparedness and alertness for making the next leap of faith required to complete the next transformative effort in a managed way, and maintain a lightness of agility.

As with any business management model, there are discrete activation points and levers associated with getting work done. In the case of the transformational organization, adaptation to transformative events can move as quickly as each person makes up their mind to participate. So the following people-levers are offered as practical ways to steer and tune the achievement of the Transformational Organization Paradigm.

LEVER 1 – Relief from dichotomy of straddling hierarchical reporting & matrix management – freeing mental capacity and confined energy.

LEVER 2 – Clarity of purpose with minimally defined expectation – self-directed people, individual meaning, and self-actuated change.

LEVER 3 – Valued contribution from intrinsic wisdom and ingenuity at all levels – new thought that goes somewhere.

LEVER 4 – Connectedness and learning though your interaction with others.

These are themes threaded throughout the Transformational Organization Paradigm and the remainder of this book.

SPEED – THE NEW PRIMARY BUSINESS RISK

"It is better to be 80% correct and make the change happen than to be 100% correct after the opportunity has passed. Most shareholders won't accept the excuse a professional football coach gave after his team lost a close game: 'We didn't lose; we just ran out of time.'"

— Norman R. Augustine, Harvard Business Review 1997

Speed trumps all other risks in the New Millennium and has a financial impact. Organizations cannot wait to stabilize their organization before attempting another transformation. Rather they must seek to destabilize it but remain functioning so that change can be injected in-stride. Furthermore, traditional analytical approaches are much too slow, organizations must move while truths are still true. This approach is as much about positioning for the next transformation as it is about maintaining viability – and the organization must regain the ground lost if transformative efforts fall short of the mark. The next transformation has even farther to go to maintain the organizations viable position.

Under both Industrial Age and Information Age paradigms, analysis has been the rudder for fiscal responsibility and financial controls, and not without its warts when it comes to the influence of individual board and executive members. Analysis serves a purpose under the Transformational Organization Paradigm but does not take centre stage the way it has in the past two decades.

Innovation is often impossible to justify. The more innovative the direction you are taking, the more difficult it is to prove. There was little proof for the founding of Google, Yahoo, Facebook, or YouTube, or the telephone or the internal combustion engine, or Tupperware, or any of the inventions that resulted from asking the question: What If...?.

Approximating the transformational target is the order of the day, particularly when it comes to maintaining speed and agility while delivering to meet consumer expectations. Have an idea what the transformed state should look like - think of initiating and executing transformative initiatives as if you are making a movie: rely on the creative expertise of the people, expect them to come up with the right solution at the appropriate time, rely on them to do what matters now in full collaboration, accepting that a fair amount of work will end up on the cutting room floor, knowing that what does could not have been anticipated through analysis and should rightly have been cut. Transformation occurs at the right speed when it is considered creative work.

The New Millennium is a time for taking unexpected directions and going off-road in attempts to find transformative solutions. Trying to justify or prove the validity of the direction takes more time than the window of opportunity allows for, and so a reliance on human ingenuity, expertise and intrinsic wisdom are indicated ways to succeed. An element of taking the commitment of the abilities of people on faith is present in the successful transformational organization. The application of more minds – in fact all minds - is necessary for transformation to be realized. And this is much different and appears to be more time consuming than change coming down through hierarchical command. However, nothing is further from the truth because since transformation (and through continuous transformation all business) is a creative endeavor in the New Millennium, command, control and even competition hinder progress and slow things down. And this is where most organizations find themselves today: stuck between collaborative creativity and command and control; losing ground fast; burning through capital funding on transformation project at alarming rates.

As much as speed of adaptation is a huge factor in business success, it only seems dramatically so under the shadow of Industrial Age, Hierarchical thinking and methods. Once the shift into the new paradigm described in this book is in hand, both work and change flow at a comfortable speed. In other words, *allowing* the work has a different time-presence than *controlling* the work. Accepting error and uncertainty as 'normal' presents a gentler and more focussed use of time. Confidence that innovation will show the way and presents opportunities for next moves in a way and magnitude that fear of failure can't.

THE TENETS of the TRANSFORMATIONAL ORGANIZATION PARADIGM

After a discussion about the sociological and psychological theories behind the Transformational Organization Paradigm, and how they leverage achievement of New Millennium business operation we must come down to a practical level to set the stage for the remainder of this book.

The following chapters deal in a detailed description of what a transformational organization looks like and what you are aiming for when attempting to achieve its characteristics. Additionally, before reading further about each of the tenets of the Transformational Organization Paradigm, it is important to convey the following core beliefs that are central to the Transformational Organization Paradigm:

1. Asking and answering the really hard questions must be felt as a thirst for knowledge at all levels in order to achieve transformational change.
2. Conflict and challenge are another form of support for transformation.
3. Managing, leading, and working in a sea of unknowns for a sustained period of time is totally possible.
4. Transformation happens the moment that each person understands the meaning it has for them as an individual.
5. Vision is realized and begins to function when each person claims and their purpose in the transformed environment.
6. The organization must achieve some of the shift to *be* in the New Millennium mindset before transforming and more of the shift while transforming.

The remaining chapters work through the following tenets of the Transformational Organization Paradigm:

1. Master Change Intelligence
2. Eradicate Paradigm-Shift Ambivalence
3. Navigate Paradoxes
4. Embrace Error
5. Acknowledge Complexity and Scale
6. Build-in the Breakdown
7. Thrive in Greyscale
8. Disperse Transformational Leadership

9. Move Forward in Leaps of Faith
10. Synchronously Co-Create the Future

The practiced ease with which the above are conducted across the organization indicates the successful achievement of the Transformational Organization Paradigm. But before launching into the details of each of the tenets, some general descriptions of what it looks like when you are 'there' with the Transformational Organization paradigm are offered below.

- You know you are 'there' when the percentage of people in the organization who lag behind adopting the tenets are few in number and often the same individuals.
- You know you are 'there' when almost no one says "most people are motivated by security and avoid responsibility" and the prevailing assumption is "work that aligns with a person's desire to contribute in a meaningful way generates a feeling of accountability and unleashes the ingenuity required to transform".
- You know you are 'there' when nobody minds operating in an uncertain environment,
- You know you are 'there' when managers and supervisors are not stretched to make a connection with their staff - when attention is not an expense or payment, but rather a substance that flows like water nourishing all seeds of thought.
- You know you are 'there' when social development within the workplace is fully integrated and not a separate activity.
- You know you are 'there' when technology serves to erode the separation between teams, functions and people.
- You know you are 'there' when merger, acquisition and divestiture activities surface the entrepreneurial and collaboration skills of management and staff rather than pit them against each other.
- You know you are 'there' when no amount of effort is so great as to be inappropriate – everyone 'goes all the way there'.
- You know you are 'there' when value networks are commonplace and tangible, when relationships are co-operative, and teams are

made up of individuals with more than one of the skillsets required to not only do the job but also develop others.

- You know you are 'there' when discussion between workers describes rather than prescribes and when multi-disciplinary / inter-disciplinary approaches are commonplace.
- You know you are 'there' when the organization is visualized month to month, there are no generally accepted rules for success, and it is normal that what worked in March may be scrapped in May.
- You know you are 'there' when information integration is valued above all, and decision making is democratized and based on future trending which is instantly availability.
- You know you are 'there' when chain of command communication only clarifies what people already fundamentally understand.
- You know you are 'there' when major changes flow through the organization without putting operations in conflict with them.

As a last word before getting into more detail, Transformational Leadership [Burns 1978/Bass 1992-2002] is a particularly necessary ingredient to the achievement of the Transformational Organization Paradigm.

In practical terms, the work of Transformational Leadership centres on opening a space for change to occur by constructing a chain of individualized, meaningful commitments to transformational work. Transformational Leadership practices, when applied to complement transformative initiatives and lift the prevailing business paradigm, have the potential to ...

- stitch together holes left by past incomplete change, and dissipate backlogged change,
- mobilize the latent and untapped inner resources of executive, management and staff,
- harvest and redistribute adaptive wisdom around the organization, and
- construct a pushing-off point for ongoing lean, agile, and innovative operations.

Under the Transformational Organization Paradigm, Transformational Leadership motivates repeated leaps of faith among superiors, peers and directly reporting workers to carve out a road to the transformed state where none existed before.

Master Change Intelligence |

The subject of business change has undergone a reframing of sorts over the last decade. Organizational behaviour and organizational development experts have referred to Change Resiliency as a desirable competency approaching the New Millennium as it relates to employees and leaders dealing with highly complex working environments. Psychologists have recently coined the term Change Immunity to describe a primal fear response to changes in the status quo – as part of human nature. These terms apply well to the change-plateau-change model of altering business, but have even more significance when put into a context of business transformation.

With change bumping up to a relentless, pervasive, and rapid fire norm rather than being an occasionally disruptive exception, it might be time to adjust the terminology we use. The terms Change Capability and Change Capacity are relatively new and approach the scope of transformation at an enterprise level where Change Capability refers to the presence of human resiliency to change combined with the practice and process maturity for Change Management across the organization – and where Change Capacity refers to the presence of human resource hours, and funding availability relative to that required for the volume of change to be pulled through and operationalized. Both are excellent measures the organization can use to gauge the practicality of strategic plans and set expectations about how quickly and how well the organization might transform.

What is missing from the equation, though, is a recognition that transformational change demands that people create the change to a great degree while they absorb and operationalize the changes. The fact is that transformation must be co-created and is not something that is 'done to' people. So, this book uses a new term to refer to the combination of skills, understandings, knowledge and personal competencies an individual must have in order to successfully rise to transformative events, and to continuously co-create transformative change. This term is *Change Intelligence*.

For the purposes of the Transformational Organization Paradigm, the term Change Immunity is expanded to include not only a clinging to the status-quo, but considering that it also extends to an addiction to Industrial Age thought and methods, and refers to the numbing effect that change fatigue and change backlog have on people.

Mastering Change Intelligence is a growth pathway for ongoing efforts to expand the capacity for transformational change among the organizations' people at executive, management and staff levels, across all lines of business and business functions. Professional development in this area cultivates an ability to absorb and adapt to continuous and broadly defined transformative mandates, and generate meaningful decisions, value-oriented ingenuity and innovation in return.

From a psychological point of view, a foundation of Emotional Intelligence and Social Intelligence is developed in combination with efforts to increase Change Resiliency. At essence, the increase of Change Resiliency and the decrease of Change Immunity within the organization enables the mastery of Change Intelligence and reciprocally leverages both Change Capacity and Change Capability.

Adding context to the mastering of Change Intelligence, the following statements summarize the fundamentals that the achieving mastery of Change Intelligence revolves around:

- Change Capacity and Change Capability are inter-related and affected by Change Resiliency and Change Immunity
- Change Immunity is an addiction to the status quo and numbness to change
- Change Resiliency is a function of Emotional Intelligence and Social Intelligence
- Intrinsic wisdom and intrinsic motivation play a big part in co-creation of the innovative solutions needed to transform
- Stasis is seen as an indicator of organizational ill-health
- Flux is seen as an indicator that transformative drivers are in the process of being addressed

CHANGE CAPACITY AND CHANGE CAPABILITY

The capability of the organization to adapt and change is directly related to the capacity of the organization to take change in and convert it to proficiency. Capability has to do with speed and efficiency of adaptation where Capacity has to do with the physical implementation of change and conversion of change into business benefits. One cannot move without the other and the more recognized the interaction between change capability and change capacity is at all levels of the organization the more effective the engine of transformation becomes.

Change Capacity in the Transformational Organization Paradigm is a measure of the skills and competencies of people such that they anticipate and have an appetite for change. It is founded in an individual desire to do work that matters, create solutions using available resources that benefit the business and peers, and harvests valuable experience. Most circles refer to this as Enterprise Change Management, Professional Development and Leadership Development.

Change Capability in the Transformational Organization Paradigm is built into the tools, methods and practices at an enterprise level. The *flexibility* and *extensibility* of the tools, methods, and practices to adapt to change offer a rudder for rightly oriented development and innovation that are built at the enterprise level for the purpose of guiding the efforts of executive, management and staff. Most circles refer to this as one or more kinds of Enterprise Architecture.

In modern terms, the existence of Enterprise Architecture gets no traction until transformation leaders construct an understanding and context for it with their people and have Change Management experts implement it. The separation of the two concepts of Change Capacity and Change Capability in this book might not align with other schools of thought, however, many organizations going down the EA path are finding that the *people* part of the EA equation still gets lost in favor of the more black and white and tangible tools, methods and practices part of the EA equation. Because EA is a transformative lever, Change Management efforts can easily fall short when it comes to raising the thoughts of the people to the higher sensibility that EA represents, focussing only on how the work is done differently.

So, when we talk about the work required to achieve the Transformational Organization Paradigm, we are approaching the entire body of Enterprise Architecture methods and practices AND the Change Capacity and Change Capability across the organization. We are elevating performance in these areas by increasing Change Resiliency and decreasing Change Immunity and applying Transformational Leadership techniques(discussed in a later chapter) to open a space for this to occur. Applied selectively, based on expert assessment and consultation, a moderate effort in this regard creates a ripple effect, tipping the balance of Change Capacity and Change Capability in the right measures for transformation to occur.

CHANGE IMMUNITY AS AN ADDICTION TO THE STATUS QUO

Psychologists refer Change Immunity as a fear response to change that is a natural instinctive and primal safety mechanism that alerts a person to take some kind of action. This mechanism repels change as a first response and sees it as a threat – something to be avoided. In business, the definition of Change Immunity expands to include the numbing effect of unrelenting change and backlogged change, and when we consider Change Immunity in terms of transformation, the term is stretched farther to define a phenomenon where an addiction to the status quo exists.

Most thought around business change management refers to Change Immunity and status quo addiction as separate conditions, but in a context of transformation, these become inseparable and must be addressed as one. That is, if we treat Change Immunity as an addiction when working to develop continuous transformation capability in the organization, we will improve both status quo addiction AND the numbing effect of change fatigue. In the process we will develop a portion of Emotional Intelligence – the portion required to move beyond the fear response.

Taken to an extreme, the transformational organization considers all change to be a life-enriching thing. *Change* and *meaning* and *value* and *fulfillment* go together as part of human development and in a transformative setting. They are inseparable. This fundamental truth indicates the way forward in reducing Change Immunity such that the emotional balance present within transforming organizations must be positively affected for transformation to occur. In reverse, if the prevalent behaviour is to deflect transformative change then the personal meaning and value an executive, manager or staff person places on their participation tilts in favor of holding to the status quo and transformation becomes very difficult to accomplish.

Reasons Change Immunity as we have described it can be considered an addiction:

1) Industrial Age command and control, and separation of people thinking and methods are deeply embedded such that employees

are discouraged from co-creating change among themselves or in collaboration for fear of losing their livelihood (safety).

2) Carrot and stick [Transactional] leadership has created a dependency on the organization for a definition of success and failure at and individual level and made competition rather than collaboration a foundation for achievement.

3) Employees are so immersed in the current organizational paradigm that they are unable to see other ways to accomplish change regardless of how compelling the transformative demand is.

For the most part, though, Change Immunity exists as part of the fabric of our still largely paternalistic society - the mechanisms of which been in place for the last 5000 years. Paternalistic methods sought to separate people from each other and from information in order to maintain order, safety and control – it is characterized by: ridged thinking; strict hierarchy; few in charge of the welfare of the many; a focus of the energies of masses/staff on minutia; the concepts of winners and losers; and the requirement of earning ones place in society through conformity. Paternalistic values focus on stability with conquest as a way of expansion and growth. The working framework of the paternalistic societal structure produced the civilized society we live in today, based in justice and standardized governance.

In business the patriarchal mindset is reflected in the aspects of professional growth that involve competition and the fear of loss (of status or financial reward). In particular, at the higher levels of the organization, do or die consequences are emphasized that serve to homogenize thought. And typically executives in Pre-Millennium organizations find themselves under threat of being cut should they communicate differently or lead their people differently than the ways they have done which led them to their position.

With so much invested by person and enterprise in old ways of thinking and doing, even the most innovative and independent thinking of us can not clearly see how we conform to and resist change. A reminder of behaviors that are consistent with addiction is in order at this point to tie the concepts above together.

Behavioral evidence that the phenomenon of Change Immunity can be considered addictive behaviour includes:

- When pressed with sound reasons to change the individual will fiercely defend the status quo and express the threats to the introducing person and the organization.
- The effort to change is equated with the pain of withdrawal from the status quo rather than the known and unknown benefits the change will bring to enrich their lives.
- Although careful counsel is given, the individual who knows they must change will still be ambivalent about it to the point of shutting down completely or acting in damaging or highly emotional ways.

And so, we are all to some degree or other addicted to [patriarchal] Industrial Age thinking and methods, and have developed an immunity to change as a result of the ways in which we have been recognized and rewarded, directly or indirectly, overtly or covertly, formally and informally over generations.

Each of us has the ability to scan our environment for the subtle and obvious cues to survival and betterment that demand a personal change. Executives have achieved their success based on a finely tuned set of skills adapted to increase their value in the environment as they understand it. However, in this transformative time, the success recipe alters radically along with the radical changes in the environment. Future success can't be predicated on past examples of successful behavior and so in a transformational setting executives prove to have the most difficulty breaking the addiction to the status quo.

Managers are rewarded for throughput of work amidst the confluence of old and new influences. They are successful when they balance the demands upon their people in any environment including a transforming one. Their day to day choice between disruptive change for a future betterment and lagging or avoiding change for the stability of throughput is magnified under transformative change. And in matrix managed environments, the role of the manager in balancing focus for throughput is exponentially more complex and therefore the natural immunity to change can grow into an addiction to the status quo. The managers response to transformative change is often to hold tighter and tighter to the status quo as a tether to some sound 'reality' that is 'manageable'.

Meanwhile staff dodge the bullets of what *is* demanded vs. *their interpretation* of that demand while continuously seeking ways to feel fulfilled, grow, be recognized, correct the 'wrongs' they see in the status quo on their own terms and resist changes that they do not see as being in alignment with what they would do to correct the 'wrongs'. Buffeted by wave upon wave of change that they have no personal attachment to, and make little sense to them, staff hold to that set of activities which they believe continues their ability to sustain themselves and their family. Torn between the demand to create transformation and meet performance evaluation metrics that don't express what they must do to create transformation, the centuries of indoctrination win out. More pressure to change more firmly presses staff into an addiction to the status quo and a numbness to change.

Like addictions to substances, addiction to the status quo is a highly charged attachment of our will to something external that has an element of need associated with it. And, to say that we are a society founded in an addiction to fear itself is not much of a stretch. Fear has been a primary motivator in businesses, in advertising, in education, in family systems and in personal achievement. Few could escape the effects. So the Transformational Organization Paradigm proposes that we approach the reduction of Change Immunity through methods that work well in breaking addiction and overcoming fear. The transformational organization begins by applying fear-oriented tactics less and less in its management and leadership practices – a significant part of which is to create a safe environment for 'error' to occur and be managed which will be discussed in a later chapter.

The transformational organization then embeds modern psychology tools that deal with addiction recovery in leadership techniques. These encourage the challenging of assumptions across the board as a way to get to the core of what is holding its people back from developing more and more capability to devise and implement transformative solutions. Leaders apply these techniques to surface and develop the apparent discrepancies of thought and belief within their people and work with individuals to resolve these so that ambivalence does not take hold and immobilize transformative work.

The work described here amounts to disassembling a system of belief that protects us from our fears and anxieties. As such it's a job that has to be approached holistically from all angles at the same time if it is to be replaced with a larger commitment to a transformational paradigm.

> *"Not being able to change doesn't mean we're lazy, stubborn, or weak. A pair of Harvard educators [Kegan and Lahey] argue that our best-laid plans often fall through for smart, self-protective (and ingeniously hidden) reasons"*

> - Oprah Winfrey Magazine 2009.

STASIS AS AN INDICATOR OF ILL-HEALTH

Before discussing the development of Change Resiliency, it is important to emphasize the effect that stasis has on the organization in the New Millennium business environment.

Attaching business growth and performance to the finite world of finance has provided a solid static measuring stick for success up until the turn of the millennium. Going forward, though, to attach success almost exclusively to something so finite is unwise, and as our financial advisors fade back to a second tier gate keeper or at least on par with innovation metrics, new advisors come to the fore and a power struggle can be expected. It's nothing new that financial control and creativity are polar-opposite viewpoints that present a fundamental but powerful paradox that the organization must balance.

For the transformational organization, the friction between these opposite mindsets creates a fertile ground for identifying whether or not the organisation is transforming. A feeling of moving into a familiar comfort zone probably means your organization is listening too much to financial advisors, backsliding into the old paradigm, and forward motion is slowing.

In pre-millennium business models, successes were often built on efforts to attract no attention in the financial game of management by maintaining an even and consistent budget expenditure and calm predictable throughput of work. Where lights-on activities are concerned this is, perhaps, still valid. However, the New Millennium business model expects ups and downs and wide swings of budget and activity and this should be considered an indicator that transformation is occurring.

Conversely, stasis can be identified by a combination of fluctuations in expenditure and a marked absence of development of new knowledge capital. Realizing waves of new knowledge capital represents the effect of moving transformative work forward through the sea of unknowns naturally associated with transformation, which will be discussed in later chapters. New waves of knowledge capital can only be realized through the process of breaking down or breaking through current or previous functional capability. So, putting a fine point on it, if your organization is experiencing few fluctuations in budget expenditure, little friction between leaders of innovation and finance leaders, few experiences of breakdown, and few shakeups surrounding organizational assumptions and founding truths, you are in stasis, and also in big trouble.

The transformational organization looks upon pockets of stasis in its organization with skepticism and seeks to uncover the forces that are keeping them that way rather than overlook the matter and assume all is well. The transformational organization inverts it's thinking where stasis is concerned. It assumes 'calm' is a red flag, and that something is not working to the benefit of the organization when stasis persists.

FLUX AS AN INDICATOR THAT NEEDS ARE BEING ADDRESSED

Modern systems have the capability to finely report on fluctuations in spend and progress against plan. For the foreseeable future an organization in flux can be interpreted as an organization that is rising to meet new needs, as they emerge, in an organic way that ultimately most efficiently serves the organization.

Forward motion at all costs is the new success imperative. And the friction points, eruptions of emotion, and guesswork that make up the fabric of rapid and radical change that is transformation, are at odds with long-steeped Industrial Age interpretation of 'safety' and 'success'.

The appearance of flux is aligned with the iterative and trial-and error and incremental approaches to work that are indicative of the ingenuity, innovation, and co-creation habits of the Transformational Organization Paradigm. New truths gestate and are birthed at all points through the transformation lifecycle that shake assumptions and what were foundational beliefs within the organization.

In balancing the effects of the intentional unbalancing of the organization, a broad indicator of success is whether or not 'flux' is the prevalent state of each team, business unit, function or line of business. When 'flux' is the prevalent state leaders and staff can feel comfortable that the organization is headed in the right direction, and will experience growth. When flux is combined with speed, and the new trajectory the result is transformation.

So, when your organization is constantly changing, delivering in new ways quickly, experiencing steady or growing consumer satisfaction, recovering rapidly from transformational breakdowns and disruptions, and talking about the reformulation of business rules and assumptions all the time without judgement or blame, interpret these tendencies indicators that your organization is living the Transformational Organization Paradigm.

There is a lot of talking, writing, messaging, trending and meeting required to support sustained flux. Spit-balling, batting ideas around, and formal brainstorming and solutions sessions, and coming to conclusions that my only be transient must keep the transformational values and objectives in mind globally and locally. This work demands that people have faith in each other, creating the space for ingenuity and creativity to surface freely in the right timing.

CHANGE RESILIENCY DEVELOPMENT

> *"Learn by going where to go"*
>
> - Theodore Roethke

Resiliency researcher, Albert Siebert, author of *The Resiliency Advantage and The Survivor Personality*, has this to say about internal psychological resilience:

> *"Resilience is the process of successfully adapting to difficult or challenging life experiences. Resilient people overcome adversity, bounce back from setbacks, and can thrive under extreme, on-going pressure without acting in dysfunctional or harmful ways. The most resilient people recover from traumatic experiences stronger, better, and wiser."*

There are many schools of thought where change resiliency is concerned. For the purposes of characterizing the transformational organization, Change Resiliency is the ability of the people of the organization to maintain solid footing and be both productive and grow personally and professionally during times of dramatic unceasing change.

In real terms, the matter of change resiliency comes down to having faith in the profound knowledge and intrinsic wisdom of others while boldly contributing one's own profound knowledge and intrinsic wisdom to the matter at hand and one's own personal success. At each step along the transformation path, the solutions needed to generate appropriate forward motion are within the work environment and its people. And a fundamental rule for forwarding transformational efforts is that: One thing leads to another – always, inevitably, and without fail.

39

Change Resiliency is an entirely people-oriented aspect that has to do with seeing the opportunities within the changes and harnessing these equally for personal and professional growth, and for the benefit of peers and the organization. Change Resiliency is a skill that can be cultivated and developed.

The transformational organization cultivates Change Resiliency among its people and couples this cultivation with reduction of fear-based motivation techniques and increase in rewarding of ingenuity. It makes requests of its people with respect and deference to the knowledge and wisdom they have to bring to the continued success of the enterprise in full knowledge that if people feel pushed to do something they won't put their whole self into it. By doing so, the Transformational Organization opens a pathway for its people to bring their best game each day.

In some respects this approach flies in the face of efforts to implement structured methods and practices across the organization, for if we are asking people to make use of what is at hand to accomplish both the change piece and the delivery piece in tandem, they may not choose to employ what we currently consider best practices or prescribed methodologies. And so a balance between the kind of transformational self-efficacy described above and the enforcement of standards, methods, and practices must be achieved. For the purposes of the Transformational Organization Paradigm, when self-efficacy wanes, the team leans on standards, methods and practices to hold ground and regroup while new ways to move forward are inspired.

Going a step farther, the development of Change Resiliency should have the goal of shortening or eliminating 4 of the 5 stages of loss (Kubler-Ross 1969) and 4 of the 5 stages of change (James O. Prochaska 2006), moving more directly from event to acceptance and event to action (respectively). There are strong emotions associated with change, it is the attachment of the person to the status quo business environment and motivational model that creates these strong emotions – which in turn creates a dependency. More specifically, it is the associated interpretation of change as stressful, dangerous, and irrational and also exciting, liberating, and affirming that deadlocks strong emotions into ambivalence.

The transformational organization has an abundance of people that do not feel as though they have settled for less than they deserve by dedicating a large part of their day to the organization. It does have an abundance of people that attend their work environment with a healthy detachment that allows them to look at events with objectivity. The people of a transformational organization come to work to do their work because it matters. It matters to them and it matters to their peers to whom they feel a fealty and respect. And, it matters to the organization which promotes a full use their talents and intellect and natural abilities day to day.

Workers who cultivate Change Resiliency within themselves are those who rarely experience high levels of stress regardless of the circumstances. Their internal struggle of whether to participate, support or commit to a change is minimal and amounts to whether to emphasize this aspect or that aspect for personal growth and contribution to the greater good. They are focussed on whether and how to express their wisdom about the implications of the changes to assist in solving the problem the change is designed to address, or else minimize the barriers and effort to bring the change into operation.

EMPHASIS OF CHANGE INTELLIGENCE MASTERY

Change Intelligence as a competency makes use of certain Emotional Intelligence and Social Intelligence principles related to moving past the fear response, learning from others, self-efficacy, seeing the larger picture, and avoiding co-dependent relationships in the workplace. Personnel at all levels will have a specific combination of work to do to master Change Intelligence, of course, however at the time of writing, there appears to be an typical emphasis of work required at each level in most organizations to achieve sufficient mastery of Change Intelligence to create a shift toward the Transformational Organization Paradigm. Below is an examination of these.

Change Intelligence Mastery at the Executive Level:

Emphasis: Acceptance of Cognitive Dissonance

At the executive level the main effort to master Change Intelligence revolves around the resolution of opposing belief systems resulting in a cognitive dissonance. In the context of the Transformational Organization Paradigm, the source of the disharmony is the belief that historical methods produce personal and enterprise success vs. the belief that transformation requires wholesale abandonment of historical methods. In demographic terms, Cognitive Dissonance is experienced by members of the board and executive team when long held and entrenched Industrial Age beliefs become more and more untenable while New Millennium 'Age' truths are difficult to discern, and are elusive in how they are to be applied, though they are obvious and clearly stated. Executives who are able to move through old thinking and outdated belief systems to grasp and wield New Millennium truths will find greater success, though their ideas may be brushed aside by many of their peers initially.

The results of Cognitive Dissonance at the executive level can be paralyzing delays in direction setting, insufficient magnitude of strategic response to transformative events, suffocating protection of organizational territory (or self-preservation) though withholding of knowledge, and wielding more 'stick' than 'carrot' with direct reports thereby choking off much needed ingenuity.

Successful resolution of Cognitive Dissonance in the midst of transformation at the executive level equates to transcending the impasse between conflicting belief systems as opposed to having to choose between them. That is, for the purposes of transforming the organization to meet New Millennium demands, the most expedient way of getting to the target transformed state is to move between BOTH belief systems to forward the progress of work. This effort focusses on steadily applying less and less of the old beliefs and methods in relationships, leadership techniques, and management tactics and requires that each executive keep an eye on their own tendency to create rationalizations that support the old ways of thinking while watching for this in others. It is the ultimate context switching challenge – a skill which will be much needed to succeed in the New Millennium business world.

So although the current 'leap' to New Millennium belief systems in business is a very large leap for those whose careers were built under Industrial Age belief systems, future leaps should be less and less extreme depending on how well the executive shift the critical mass of belief and value systems toward New Millennium thinking.

Naturally, this will not happen overnight. At the time of writing, the author anticipates the shifting process to take 30 years or more to complete with the law of diminishing returns active during that time. So, where the executive team is able to shift the balance of weight of its beliefs and value systems from pre-millennium to New Millennium truths, beliefs, and value systems sooner rather than later, greater viability and returns can be expected.

Characteristics of the executive who is succeeding in shifting to New Millennium belief and value systems are:

- Understands and accepts the need for change, champions the change rather than seeking stability or rationalizing the breakdown of existing belief systems
- Increases in their ability to navigate the paradox of old and new belief systems and accepts that these co-exist while constantly seeking ways to shift their own thinking and the thinking of others toward the new mindset
- Mindfully ignites new thought in others reaching through and beyond middle management to harvest intrinsic wisdom from across the organization

Change Intelligence Mastery at the Management Level:

Emphasis: Resolution of Ambivalence

Middle managers represent the confluence point between transformative vision and functional transformation realization. They are constantly in the centre of all paradoxical situations and contexts that are inherent in transformation, and are charged with holding the executive and staff accountable to the value proposition of the transformation. Paradoxically, middle managers are evaluated on their ability to produce throughput rather than champion innovation and ingenuity. In a rapidly and continuously transforming environment where ingenuity and co-creation of new knowledge capital is the primary key to success, this translates to a compounding of ambivalence on financial, human resources, and toolset fronts.

While middle managers will struggle with Cognitive Dissonance associated with a shifting centre of 'truth' in the organization they have learned to be more accepting of the so called 'moving target' having been career-raised in downsized, flattened, matrix managed organizations. Ambiguity is a more broadly accepted part of their reality as compared with executives. So, the middle manager feels less need to come to terms with a single belief system but feels more of a need to resolve the contradictory positive and negative aspects of daily transformation demands in order to appropriately and meaningfully produce throughput. They must argue both sides within themselves and manage impulses to either react impulsively or stop and wait for a break in the action (which most likely won't happen).

Managers who are successful under rapidly and consistently transforming environments break through their own ambivalence by identifying the meaning and purpose of transformational work for themselves and for their peers, superiors, and direct reports. They are able to zero in on the one or two activities that matter most in the current context, and do these activities in full knowledge that the centre of 'truth' and context for producing success will most likely change in a matter of weeks or days in some cases.

Characteristics of the middle manager who is succeeding in resolving their own ambivalence on a day to day basis are:

- Understands and accepts the need for change
- Anticipates change rather than seeking stability
- Elicits wisdom and creativity in approaching changes spherically
- Rewards ingenuity and innovation

- Taylors the meaning of the transformation for the unit or function or program
- Specific about what is being asked in terms of changed behavior
- Defines the recursive properties of the transformation
- Socializes new ideas and possible shifts at all times regardless of whether they are expected to manifest or not
- Seeks commentary on anticipated changes in the moment
- Adds context to the changes as they see it
- Identifies ambivalence about the change and moves through it while coaching others to do the same
- Accepts and harnesses the power of error

Change Intelligence Mastery at the Staff Level:

Emphasis: Translation of Critical Thinking Into Ingenuity

At the staff level an equal amount of activity in shifting of thinking is required to support a transformational environment. Later chapters discuss synchronous communication and co-creation of transformation, and these are an essential part of mastering Change Intelligence. In particular staff must move past the fear-based thinking associated with lingering Industrial Age management and leadership techniques, working to view the changing context of their day to day work with healthy detachment and objectivity. The transformational message, in its efforts to stimulate a sense of urgency can often trigger Change Immunity. The more the transformational message is heard, the harder it is for staff to come out from under the curtain of fear of failure and transformational breakdowns can trigger.

Staff who try to regain a perceived loss of stability in their work environment through wave after wave of transformative change quickly burn out. Industrial Age-fostered behavioural tendencies toward competition and blame that separate person from person can be extremely difficult to discard at the staff level regardless of how wanted the transformed state. A desire to make sense of their environment must be discarded in favor of an attitude of adventure and valued contribution.

Developing skills around critical thinking have assisted the elevation of staff self-efficacy in ever flattening organizations and these new skills must do more than question and assess, they must yield ingenious solutions and pathways that generate forward motion regardless of whether this change or that change comes to pass, or this truth or that truth still exists tomorrow. There is a distinct incisiveness and keen perceptiveness to develop that can only surface along with a sense of having valuable knowledge and abilities to contribute for the mutual benefit of the company and the individual.

Staff who are successful under rapid unrelenting change have an attitude of not having to prove what works or is worthy of investment before communicating new ideas. They know there are a million ways to get things done and there is no longer a need to wade through hoops to be heard. They take themselves and what they have to offer seriously enough to break any dependency on punitive/incenting response as a motivator of performance.

Characteristics of the staff member who is succeeding in applying critical thinking to produce ingenuity are:

- Understands and accepts the need for change
- Anticipates change rather than seeking stability
- Understands that one thing inevitably leads to another
- Consistently open to new wisdom and creativity in approaching work
- Seeks to contribute ingenuity and make innovative proposals spherically (upward and outward)
- Internalizes the meaning of the change for themselves their peers and who they report to
- Specific about what is being proposed and how it contributes to transformational objectives regardless of whether their message embraces the 'party line'
- Identifies the emergence of forming changes that are ready to be integrated with operation
- Identifies when transformative changes are realized and provides advice to peers and who they report to

- Seeks commentary on anticipated changes in the moment
- Adds context to the changes as they see it
- Identifies ambivalence about the change and moves through it

Change intelligence mastery is an unceasing effort that occurs on an individual level, reinforced by team and group dynamics that are oriented around group genius and synchronous ingenuity which are discussed in later chapters. Not everyone in your organization will master change intelligence, and it may not be advisable for this to be the case. The objective should be to maintain a balance of individuals at each level of the organization who have a demonstrated mastery of the elements of change intelligence.

CHAPTER SUMMARY

Master Change Intelligence Tenet - Central Concepts
- There is a reciprocal relationship between Change Capacity and Change Capability. The more you have of one, the more you can develop of the other.
- There is an inverse relationship between Change Resiliency and Change Immunity. The more you reduce Change Immunity the greater the Change Resiliency is possible in the organization.

Characteristics of the Transformational Organization
- Understands and accepts the need for continuous change as part of the modern business environment. Anticipates change rather than seeks stability. Keeps an eye on the horizon for new change to be adapted to.

As it Appears In Communication
- Describes the transformative event and corresponding adaptation required in broad terms
- Directs people to feedback mechanisms
- Asks for what changes are anticipated for each unit or function or program
- Defines the recursive

As it Appears In Leadership
- Socializes new ideas and possible shifts at all times regardless of whether they are expected to manifest or not
- Seeks commentary on anticipated changes in the moment
- Adds context to the changes as they see it

properties of the change

- Connects feedback received to see how it reflects the transformation adaptation strategy
- Taylors the meaning of the change for the unit or function or program
- Specific about what is being asked in terms of changed behavior

- Identifies ambivalence about the change
- Asks for the meaning of the change for the people involved individually
- Encourages individuals to come to terms with changes through conversation
- Elicits wisdom and creativity in approaching changes
- Rewards ingenuity and innovation

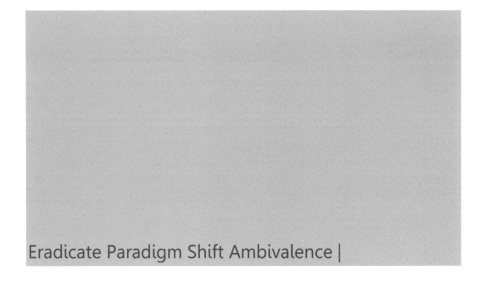

Eradicate Paradigm Shift Ambivalence |

"It's like the company is undergoing five medical procedures at the same time," he told me. "One person's in charge of the root-canal job, someone else is setting the broken foot, another person is working on the displaced shoulder, and still another is getting rid of the gallstone. Each operation is a success, but the patient dies of shock."

– Jeanie Daniel Duck, Harvard Business Review on Change 1998

An examination of the occurrence and effect of ambivalence across the organization is important when discussing continuous transformation and achieving the Transformational Organization Paradigm because it is one of two keys that unlock forward motion in substantial volumes. The other key is the application of Transformational Leadership techniques discussed in a later chapter. This chapter zeros in on the nature and triggers of ambivalence when it comes to business and organizational transformation before talking about how elevating the thought paradigm acts to root out ambivalence. Ambivalence due to straddling Industrial Age and Information Age methods and thinking must be explored before discussing transformation paradox resolution, and the embracing of 'error' in the next chapters.

Ambivalence can spread from person to person, team to team, and department to department as it is easier for staff raised in lingering command and control environments to be fearful of change and ambiguity than it is for them to hold a confident curiosity about it. In fact, a necessary indoctrination to feel fear in the face of uncertainty has been fostered by Industrial Age methods – that is to say, the intention of these methods has been to separate and immobilize people until clear command and instruction is given so that the environment is predictable and direct-able. Even at the most senior levels, this indoctrination is profoundly rooted and few people in any organization can see clearly, through the ingrained cloud of fear, worry and doubt to mobilize their own resources and the resources of other people.

Whether at the executive, department, team or individual level, allowing ambivalence to take hold is deadly in the New Millennium. Each of us must unlearn what we have learned about management, leadership and driving success, and challenge others to do the same. Transformation demands a markedly different approach to progressing work than bulldozing through change after change or leading a charge to push change through. Furthermore, doing so has proven to yield less than optimal success and resulted in a good deal of stress and burnout at all levels of the organization. A deep shift in how we regard and respond to uncertainty and ambiguity must take place – and the work to gain ground in disallowing ambivalence and maintain a growing balance of ambivalence reduction will be a constant effort in most organizations in the decades ahead.

Not only does the ambivalence immobilize the application of effort to work at hand, it immobilizes ingenuity and creativity as well. In practical terms, this is evidenced at all levels by a reluctance to speak and act genuinely for fear of making waves, losing credibility, or being seen as vulnerable. These are behaviours not typically associated with ambivalence, but in fact they are defensive mechanisms that protect a personal territory from the perceived threat of change, however rational and justified that change is.

An opposite viewpoint must be cultivated that reads:

Fear ambivalence for it foreshadows stasis and stagnation; celebrate the discomfort of change for it breathes new life into the environment and exercises mental muscle needed for ingenuity and forward motion.

Enculturating this viewpoint is no small hill to climb.

CRESTING THE HILL

We sit in a suspended state between and past human culture and future human culture. Past human culture was founded in an addiction of sorts to the status quo fostered by management methods involving power over others, withholding natural rewards for well-intended effort, and motivating with carrot-and-stick tactics. Future human culture is founded in pursuit of the deepest and most genuine possible expression of one's abilities, offered freely for use by others in an exchange aimed at the maturation of ideas and concepts into productive elements to meet constantly transforming environmental challenges and opportunities.

In order to make a leap to the optimal transformational organization, an intervention of sorts is required to create a clear point from past to future. A natural withdrawal can be expected as organizations go through this process in addition to the same kinds of machinations commonly associated with addiction. Organizations that wish to operate in a transformational way can benefit greatly by adapting techniques that psychology professionals use to treat substance addiction – addressing and resolving the ambivalence and cognitive dissonance associated with the addiction to sameness and certainty.

Poking-the-bear of addiction to the Industrial Age thinking has already begun in many organizations. The nature of addiction being what it is, those most heavily addicted will fight to defend and continue their behaviour. Continuing on this line of thought, commanding someone to make a change and providing rationale for making that change in an addictive scenario usually pushes them into making an argument for staying the same. Following the most modern methods for treating addiction, use of Motivational Interviewing tactics can leverage a permanent shift through ambivalence and avoidance.

Along with pursuing the reversal of Industrial Age thinking and breaking the dependency of staff upon it, is a necessary letting go of past human culture 'triggers' for the dependency. This means that the vestures of Industrial Age command and control methods should be minimized or sidelined in favor of new management methods, for example:

- Participative organizational models replace competition
- Value chain and value network replace reward and punishment
- Knowledge workers replace strict processes and procedures that focus on minutia
- Intrinsic motivation replaces command and control
- Connectedness learning and collaborative co-creation replace separation of people and hierarchy

As the work of shifting the emphasis of command and control methods out of mainstream management practices proceeds, a second wave of push-back can be expected as organizations encounter the root of the addiction to the status quo - without stasis, command and control of workers is an inappropriate way of thinking, being or acting. Exposing command and control as obsolete doesn't mean that the methods and practices people have relied on will cease to be applied, nor that the people who have risen to success and personal achievement by applying them will go quietly.

Enter the second part of addressing the dissolution of ambivalence: drawing attention to and sometimes confronting the discrepancies in thinking between pre-millennium and post-millennium environments. In order for the organization to complete a shift to the New Millennium super-agile way of doing business, Industrial Age methods must be replaced with Information Age and New Millennium 'Age' methods. Not to do so tempts the addiction of management and staff to the status quo, stability, few unknowns etc., and prevents them from letting go sufficiently to embrace the ambiguity that already surrounds them and moving onto seeking the solutions within themselves and others that they need in order to support transformation.

So, part of cresting the hill to complete the paradigm shift toward the transformational organization is retraining valued executives, managers, and leaders in the new management and leadership styles that enable transformative and agile operation as a permanent state. In some cases this will work, in other cases, it won't and a hard look is required at who has it within their set of strengths the aptitude for making repeated leaps of faith out of a state of ambivalence again and again and who is not.

It is important to talk about commitment level when discussing making the rest of the shift to the Transformational Organization Paradigm. Motivating a leap of faith and gaining commitment are definitely connected and when we operate on one the other is affected. But there is a strictly mechanical lever here that has nothing to do with what style of management you are following or subscribing to as the prevalent people management and leadership method in your organization. Here it is:

> *People are willing to do what is asked of them, including making a leap of faith, when they feel they will be supported by their superiors, by the tools they are provided, by the funding they are allotted and failing everything else, they will be supported in making the decisions, and in applying the ingenuity that they need to in order to generate success.*

So, regardless of how the company explains, rationalizes, communicates, coaches, leads, funds or resources the transformation they ask their staff to make, staff will make that transformation only if they have been granted the authority to do so in the way they think works best. Their work will take longer or shorter to yield results based on their knowledge and experience and access to people – but they will get there.

This brings us to the pivotal point of resolving ambivalence and generating commitment at all levels...and where classic change management practices are a bit thin. In order for any one person to make a decision to change how they work and be committed enough to it to see it through, some part of the equation must have meaning to them and they must see their purpose within it. When we think about the multiple, complex, varied, rapid-fire changes that blow through each person's work and home environment week to week and month to month the matter of change becomes even more personal *and* emotional.

Different organizations will experience a heightened scale and speed of change differently, the need to motivate through team and individual intrinsic value. The necessity for everyone to be a leader does not differ either. And these two notions work well together to naturally dissipate rising ambivalence and resolve discrepancies in thinking as the shift toward a Transformational Organization Paradigm progresses.

A LONG ROW TO HOE

Using this Agricultural Age axiom to describe the rooted nature of Industrial Age management methods and organizational paradigms seems woefully inadequate in describing the work that needs to be done to re-sculpt even one organization into a New Millennium model.

It is the premise of this book that the transformations taking place across economic and social systems is a manifestation of a natural pendulum swing away from patriarchal methods that have been in place for thousands of years. Patriarchal systems of control run very deep indeed and altering, replacing, or even thinning them strikes at the very heart of what the average person considers the very construct of their existence. New Millennium evolutionary demand is like a force of nature, however, and cannot be stoppered or held at bay. There is no 'getting back to normal', however, the timing of each organizations adaptation *can* be tempered to allow for the most appropriate depth of the adjustment to be made however.

Instinctively the average person understands the magnitude of work in front of them in their work-life and home-life transformation, and faced with this overwhelming fact, they will naturally pick and choose those elements of each transformation to rise to, and which to ignore based on their personal abilities and circumstances. As an enterprise, each organization should seek to constantly encourage an alignment of what individuals and groups feel they can rise to and what the organization requires in order to transform. This effort alone denotes a significant alteration in performance measurement and capability development that is markedly different than what we have come to know as standard management and organizational development practices.

Rather than herd staff through predefined mazes of training and education, and exposure to best practices, human resource development must first cultivate self-efficacy among its people, aiming for a baseline formulated according to the nature of the business and an assessment of the distance the organization must travel to transform. Again, this step alone may be felt as threatening to management and the executive especially, many of whom have built their professional success upon traditional transactional methods of leadership, the power of persuasion, and sheer force of will.

An important paradox exists in the concepts here. For just as self-efficacy acts to dissolve ambivalence, it also catalyzes an 'everyone for themselves behaviour' which may undermine the necessary co-creation and connectedness necessary to meet New Millennium demands if not stewarded in tandem with competition reduction efforts. In fact under Industrial Age command and control scenarios, self-efficacy is converted to a separating agent which is the reverse of what is needed to be successful in the New Millennium.

So, raising self-efficacy among staff has to be accompanied by an adoption of Transformational Leadership style by management and executive, and a foundation of trust in building out participative organizational models. Furthermore, as we encourage self-efficacy as a way to extinguish ambivalence we must also allow more self-directed professional development if efforts to increase the connection points between what the organization needs and what individuals feel they can rise to are to be successful. This loosening of bonds and removal of constraints naturally inhibits ambivalence in the presence of transformative forward motion.

Developing the trust that once-burned-twice-shy staff may actually receive what they need to confidently approach the unknown and simultaneously grasp more accountability for determining their value to the organization means that the natural tendency to revert to a few people pushing things through to a larger populace must be demonstrably discouraged. So too, natural tendencies among managers to control all aspects of the work their staff is doing must be visibly discouraged, as should all forms of manipulation, turf marking, competitiveness, and the game of delayed gratification.

With fewer and fewer recognizable command and control orientation points evident and difficulties in wielding new motivational tools taking time to overcome, much support will be needed and the role of Human Resources can be expected to expand greatly. All of this demands a level of patience, selflessness, and letting go among the executive that may be agonizing. However, it is necessary to create the space and open-ness for management and staff to shoulder more of the burden of creating and re-creating the business environment though continuous transformation. Executives must do this mindfully and with purpose, leaning on Transformational Leadership methods, and constantly assessing and reassessing the context within which they are asking their management and staff to perform - never attempting to guess what those people need in order to make each transformation work nor predetermining a detailed definition of a successful outcome.

THE MITIGATING EFFECTS OF TRANSFORMATIONAL PARADIGM

Once a balance of the Transformational Organization Paradigm is achieved, a continuous ironing-out of ambivalence within the management and staff of the organization is required. Ambivalence can be a function of addiction, it can be a function of an absence of support for self-efficacy, and can also be a deeper dissonance between the requested adaptation and the values that a person or team holds. And so, ambivalence can crop up, take root, and interfere with transformative work without consistent efforts to keep it at bay or motivate people to make leaps of faith out of it.

Here is where change management as a mainstream enterprise practice and function can extremely useful. As change must pass through people to be accomplished and achieve benefits, it seems a natural fit that the enterprise change management function becomes part of the service that Human Resources provides.

The Transformational Organization Paradigm described in this book is people-centric and technology founded. The transformational organization is foremost about connecting people in precise and meaningful ways using knowledge-capital, information, and communication technologies so that co-creation and innovation occurs with ease as the organization delivers and while it continually reshapes itself.

As exhausting as it sounds to attempt to maintain a shifting of value and meaning and repositioning these constantly with the teams and individuals doing the work to achieve right-level agility, it's no more exhausting than the amount of effort it took (past tense) to maintain a strict hierarchy of command and control that was based in separating people, incenting them with delayed gratification kinds of rewards, motivating them through managed competition, and still getting the throughput required to keep the business healthy. In the past Industrial Age paradigm, the commitment, meaning and purpose were clear and simple. They were tagged to an individual and to a concept of being loyal to one's employer – the entity that provided for food, shelter and opportunities for learning. To work against this paradigm was heresy at worst, was career limiting at best and generally considered disrespectful. So revered were the layers of the hierarchy and the people who held the positions in the hierarchy that new ideas were considered a non-conformity that threatened the viability of the organization. At the height of the Industrial Age this was probably true.

Not as unlikely as it might seem, trust and faith were the lifeblood of the Industrial Age kind of loyalty just as trust and faith are the lifeblood of the Transformational Organization Paradigm and the Millennium 'Age' kind of loyalty. A difference is that each time a major change blows through the organization, a re-commitment to trust and faith needs to happen in order to maintain delivery and prepare for the next major change, and avoid ambivalence taking root amidst the ambiguity and uncertainty that constant 'flux' presents. The management and staff of the transformational organization must to be grounded in trust and faith at all times, just as they were under more static Industrial Age paradigms. The difference is that the individual working in the organization is putting as much trust and faith in their own abilities as they are in the company they work for and in the peers they work with. The New Millennium loyalty factor reaches beyond their immediate "commander" to the extended value network people work within. Under the conditions of trust and faith ambivalence is hard to maintain for any length of time.

Predictability and mentoring between peers and working toward desired outcomes in unique and creative ways are keys to clearing out ambivalence. In other words we draw out in each other the meaning and purpose of our involvement in the transformational organization. We re-commit to each other as respected professionals or disband in acknowledgement that the group no longer serves a productive purpose - redistributing to new groups and teams in need of particular expertise.

Influence is everything – but not in the traditional sense of the word. Influence is made up of the substance of the contribution by the individual in a transformational organization that either leads to the next new thought or the next action that progresses the change. In order to fulfill the 'move forward at all costs' requirement people at all levels will need to take the kind of risks that under the Industrial Age paradigm would have been seen as insubordination. Since the stakes are higher, ambivalence naturally has a harder time taking root.

CHAPTER SUMMARY

Eradicate Paradigm Shift Ambivalence Tenet - Central Concepts
- Ambivalence can be disguised in many forms: risk aversion, decision aversion, territoriality, withholding of self and information and immobilizes the organization.
- Ambivalence is an expression of an addiction to the status quo.

- Ambivalence is an expression of a lack of clarity of individual meaning and purpose of the changes on the horizon.

Characteristics of the Transformational Organization
- Continuously roots out ambivalence applying modern positive psychology methods to identify it and collaboratively work with individuals and groups to support self-efficacy and explore the decisional balance in supporting and participating in the change. Works to achieve the highest possible commitment to change at all times.

As it Appears In Communication
- Expresses empathy and understanding, seeing the situation through the eyes of the executor or the receiver of the change
- Offers ways for people to express how they will adapt to the changes
- Reflects back to the receivers an acknowledgement of challenges faced and asks open ended questions to create forward motion in thinking about the change
- Affirms the feedback received as a strength of the organization and evidence of success
- Restates the meaning for the company if the changes are not realized

As it Appears In Leadership
- Expresses business in change talk terms using Motivational Interviewing approaches
- Allows individuals and groups to express resistance without countering with rationale
- Develops the discrepancies present in the thinking of the individual or group and revisits the commitment choice until a final decision to commit or not to commit is reached
- Affirms the ability of the individual or group to embrace the change and remain competent Points out the strengths the individual or group has to apply to the challenges ahead
- Avoids fear talk and talk of negative consequences of not changing but holds the line on the necessity of the change

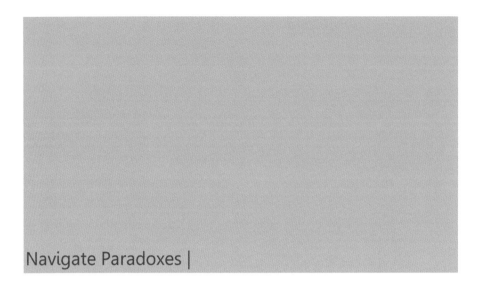

Navigate Paradoxes |

A fundamental principle of transformation and part of what makes transformation different than 'change' is that the polarization of mindset from current state to transformed state is so dramatic that the two ways of thinking are nearly impossible to consider together.

 The Transformational Organization Paradigm uses these naturally occurring paradoxes in thinking, activity, and outcome as a source of forward propulsion for transformative work. At each level of the organization affected by transformative work paradoxes of intention, demand, skillset, goal and purpose exist. Identifying these paradoxes as transformative work is approached and as they emerge over the course of the transformation initiative is typically an untapped success lever. Leaders, operational staff, and program and project team members will often be shocked into immobilization when confronted by paradoxical demands inherent in transformative work, or otherwise may have difficulty navigating the paradoxes and working through them slowing progress and increasing costs. In responding to paradoxical demands in this way, they ignore a powerful tool that may be used to move more deftly through ambiguity and uncertainty toward the transformed state.

The following diagram depicts the primary paradox of work aimed at transforming the complex organization that is straddling Industrial Age and Information Age into a New Millennium constantly transforming.

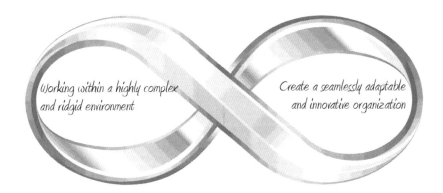

Working within a highly complex and rigid environment

Create a seamlessly adaptable and innovative organization

Additionally, paradoxes present under *continuous* transformation commonly include:

1. Develop the next change while maintaining efficient and agile operation.
2. Develop employees in a structured way while functional jurisdictions, spans of influence and reporting structures change.
3. Take time to interpret the meaning of change, failure, error and new learnings in the midst of shifting priorities and the pressure for speed of delivery.
4. Create the calm space for new thought and concept realizations to surface while tendencies to fight fires and move into survival mode distract efforts.
5. Achieve a high quality, stable and rightly designed toolset even though the requirements are changing and the tools are expected to be reinvented in the near term.

In adopting change, the moment of letting go of the old and committing to the new is exactly where optimization and benefits achievement begins. Where transformational paradoxes are concerned, many separate paradoxes will have had to be confronted and navigated before this can happen. Furthermore, the point at which the balance of paradoxes have been resolved can only be identified by the people doing the work, and so the entire focus of individual judgement and leadership is on paradox resolution and the right timing the switch to a benefits realization focus.

THE NATURE OF NAVIGATING PARADOXES

Transformative paradoxes must be taken in as a whole rather than expressed in piecemeal by individual risk items, barriers, roadblocks, issues, or resistance items. In the Transformational Organization Paradigm, paradoxes form part of the foundation of communication strategies and change management efforts for transformational work, but beyond that they are a natural part of the day to day thinking of people at all levels as a way to track transformation progress and so act as a release valve for stress. This is a key achievement characteristic for organizations adopting the Transformational Organization Paradigm.

The transformational organization maps the transformation paradoxes across the organizations formal and informal functions, groups, and teams as part of transformation strategy work. And as each program, project, task force, work package and activity is approached, the paradoxes inherent in moving from current state to transformed state are remapped at lower and lower levels.

The identification, mapping and navigation of paradoxes also forms a large part of developing change intelligence competencies related to turning unacceptable unknowns/uncertainty into acceptable unknowns/uncertainty in the minds of executive, management and staff. The greatest forward motion a transformative effort can gain is through consistently and intentionally encountering and resolving the highest friction point within each paradox.

Navigating paradoxes is work that requires each leader and team member to confront the opposing directives, thinking, activity, outcome, assumptions, intention, demand, skillset, goal or purpose within the transformation. Asking questions like these ones listed below assist in resolving transformational paradoxes:

- What assumptions prevail that keep us from learning what we need to learn in order to move forward?
- What new truth are we realizing at this point?
- What is real and harness-able at this moment that will move us forward?

- What can I think and do now that matters?

Navigating a paradox can be defined as the activity of continuously assessing the degree of swinging between two opposing necessities each of which demands 100% of the attention of the individual, and have equal weight at the time of their identification. A balance of thought and activity on either side of the paradox for any length of time halts forward motion of the transformation either immediately or through the creation of untenable circumstances down the road. Alternatively, extreme swings between the opposing aspects of the paradigm result in a consumption of time that threatens the viability of the transformative work since the more extreme the swing the more time spent in each aspect and the more recovery time required to re-centre the balance of work. The more movement that takes place within in the highest friction points of the paradox (on either side of the centre), the greater the visibility of new truths, and the faster the understanding of those truths takes place.

Holding attention on the highest friction point of the paradox can be experienced as painful and exhausting and risks stagnation there (ambivalence), however attention should not dissipate until a sense that sufficient new learning and new ways of thinking have been achieved that support letting go of the 'old' state and committing to the transformed state, whether it has been constructed fully or not. Avoidance of the friction points within transformational paradoxes is a natural tendency, and so transformation leaders must correct for this tendency in themselves and their staff, Presenting and re-presenting the paradoxes identified.

Paradoxes typically have a cyclical recursive shape. We use the infinity symbol or double-helix to represent paradoxes. The movement of the activity of navigating any paradox has a surfing back and forth pattern – like two steps forward, one step back, ebb and flow and give and take. Similar to balancing a bicycle, the back and forth motion is combined with effort to power forward motion and this metaphor should be held within the minds of people at all levels as being the optimal achievement of organizational momentum under continuous transformation. Not surprisingly, this is the same pattern as trial-and-error and iterative approaches and so it is easy to see how ignoring paradoxes or trying to constrain or eradicate them by force only serves to put the brakes on innovation and creativity, and ultimately halts transformation.

The important point here is that the recursive part of navigating the transformational paradox should not be interpreted as bad, only an opportunity to re-approach the optimum timing for entrenching changes. Education in this aspect of Change Intelligence has to be supported by all other management practices in order to work. The more pervasive command and control management methods are, and the more pervasive transactional leadership styles are, the greater the hindrance to the line of sight of right-timing transformation emergence into operation. And so these methods must be removed in order for transformational paradoxes to be navigated in a way that propels the organization forward.

Particular alternations to how project scope is managed are necessary to creating the balance points upon which the individual, group or enterprise place their footing during transformation. Trade-offs made in setting and resetting these balance points must be weighted toward what is perceived to be the nature of the next transformational wave rather than representing a deflating cut in scope when it comes time to harvest the learning from trial and error to date. There is an additional reach into the change and transition tactics that operational personnel must make to navigate the transform-while-operating paradox. Specifically, the project team must begin to speak in terms of the paradoxes that must be navigated as the functional unit co-crafts and then masters the transition of transformative changes into operation again and again. Currently, paradoxes are identified as discrete or inter-related project risks, however, describing paradoxes in terms of risk frames things in negative terms – expresses them as a danger rather than a the creative engine that they actually are.

It is best to communicate paradoxes in terms of the trade-offs and balance points each team or function must consider as the awareness of the change is developed. This dialogue forms an integral part of sketching the to-be state.

Predefined paradoxes can act as a measurement tool in assessing whether or not the organization is transforming. Discussing and documenting the number of paradoxes that were successfully navigated and how they were resolved can play a part in phase-end and post-initiative reviews. They not only reveal how well the paradoxes were identified going into the work, but also reveal fundamental shifts in belief systems and thinking that are to be built upon in future transformative initiatives. The degree to which thinking and approaches shift during a transformational initiative is a direct indicator of how successful the organization will be in executing the next transformational initiative. To put it another way, the new thought and approaches developed are somewhat less important than the increased ability to see where paradoxes lay and the ability to develop new thinking and approaches each and every time the organization transforms.

Other evidence that paradoxes are being successfully navigated includes:

- A surge of energy returns when new information surfaced by working through the friction points of the paradox and that energy leads to concrete inquiry and new direction.
- Wisdom is received in exchange for information injected into the paradox.
- New answers become clear at the right time and then naturally become obsolete as the next wave of unknowns approaches.

Energy reciprocated from the navigation of paradoxes demonstrates that the organization is transforming and at the same time, renews the commitment of individuals to the achievement of stated and revised outcomes.

IT IS IMPOSSIBLE TO GO TOO FAR

Over the last 50 years, experience with change triggered by technology has demonstrated that the possibilities for improvement and innovation are endless. However, the human factor in applying these makes or breaks the realization of innovation and improvement opportunities, and in turn affects the organizations' ability to realize the potential offered by the New Millennium business scene. The very language of transformation conveys sensing and perceiving, and a dynamic kind of resourcefulness. And, in an environment that is in a creative flux all the time, it's simply not possible to go too far in communicating, coaching and facilitating each other along.

One paradox that works in favor of New Millennium adaptation is that while constant transformation requires us to learn how to connect and reconnect with others in new ways all the time, the very connection of people with people is THE thing that accelerates adaptation. A reason for this is that the connection between people adds meaning to situations and rationale, injects value at an individual level, and offers natural immediate, rightly timed opportunities for mentoring, new learning, and support exchange. The challenges and the opportunities for growth inherent in navigating this particular paradox are the combination of qualities that define job satisfaction for most people.

A staple of the Industrial Age bag of tricks was the elusive and virtually unachievable promise that if you just make more money you will be able to do all those things that you find most personally fulfilling. This promise was systematically broken over the 1980s, and 90s through downsizing, rightsizing, automation, fair employment standards and sustainability. Quite conveniently, as demand for technology-skilled workers grows in the New Millennium and upward mobility opportunities shrink, a new professional and personal growth pathway emerges that has the potential to replace money a motivator, and resolve the question "where do we go if we can't move upward?". This occurs just in time for the coming of age of Millennials in the workforce who (demographically speaking) are value- and contribution- driven.

The awarding a greater span of influence and more supervisory and budget responsibility in exchange for good performance pales in comparison to having a channel for expressing all of our unique personal resources at work, and having the results of that effort be visible and appreciated (not that these are mutually exclusive). So long as salary is adequate, people most keenly want to be appreciated, to contribute, and to create. This desire holds true regardless of personality type, level of position, and personal background.

In navigating the paradox of structured professional development amidst continuously shifting functional expectations and jurisdiction, the executive and manager cannot apply too much facilitation, coaching and support for their direct reports, especially in eliciting ingenuity and innovation Many organizations are accustomed to a dynamic of constant interaction between staff and their line manager, however much of this is conducted in one-off verbal communication that lacks cohesiveness and sufficient depth of meaning to be effective. Additionally, the time demand of being in constant circulation in formal meetings and dynamically available to staff makes it difficult to get administrative and "project" work completed. Blocking off time in ones calendar for this is less and less feasible while the organization strains to straddle Industrial Age and Information Age paradigms that are ever moving apart. So over-communication is really important.

At the same time, the challenge put before staff day to day is to make skilled decisions, come up with solutions, and teach and learn from others to resolve paradoxes. Combined with the breadth of exposure to multiple disciplines and subject areas associated with moving from one team to another, a Participative Management approach has the potential of keeping employees engaged. So while, specialization and knowledge-driven work appears to be restrictive when it comes to professional development, it only looks that way through the lens of the remnants of Industrial Age. Essentially, there is more than enough challenging and rewarding work to keep everyone interested and committed, and part of the 'advancement' equation is developing staff with expert knowledge in more than one "specialization" area. A greater role of HR and OD&D is indicated when we combine this truth with the bandwidth shortage of the current 'line manager'.

Although an individuals' contribution is more evident in a transformational environment – with the associated upsides and downsides that come with that exposure - there is a ringing lack of competitiveness present in the Transformational Organization Paradigm.

That is, there are no "winners" and no "losers" even though there are "successes" and "failures" as people grind through the friction points of transformational paradoxes. Everyone shares in the relief of navigating paradoxes into resolution. This point cannot be stressed enough by leaders in the New Millennium.

Competition between people within organizations must be minimized for paradoxes to be resolved. Challenge presents plentiful opportunities for expression and appreciation, but competition separates people in an environment that demands that thought is are sparked through collaboration with regularity.

Earning the right to management and executive attention, and paying of 'dues' are notions that existed in plenty in the passing organisational, leadership, and management and paradigms. It will be impossible to navigate the tearing effect of transformational paradoxes without a high level of connectedness with others, and this connectedness demands that relationships between people are cohesive and free of the envy, malice, and greed that can accompany competitiveness. Well beyond chatting at the coffee station, maintaining connectedness has to do with content-rich conversations that might look like venting or complaint on the surface but are real opportunities and channels for original and corrective ideas and thoughts to be harvested, matured, and applied to the resolution of paradoxes.

SHIFT IN THE PLACE OF INFORMATION TECHNOLOGY

Information Technology has been seen to be a culprit in the causality of transformation and this is at once true and untrue. Information technologies have arisen from a demand to harness the power of processing the increasing masses of information for a growing global population. In developing IT, we have come to a point where we can perceive what potential there is in having technology tools alleviate more and more of the burden of mundane repetitive work in our personal lives, and in business.

Regularly and in ever tightening cycles, Information Technology has raised the bar on what an individual can accomplish in a day, what an individual can demand of the suppliers it deals with each day, and what an individual can demand from their employer each day. In turn the freedoms and empowerments spawned from the paradox of doing more with less in business create a new paradox that must be navigated on every level of the organization, in all functions and amidst all teams and groups. Failure to embrace and then navigate the following paradox results in a drag on corporate resources and drains the capability of the organization to generate ingenuity and co-create the transformed state.

The paradox of Information Technology has been assumed to be the trigger for business transformation, however the truth is that the IT paradox is the primary energy source for transformation that is triggered by an evolutionary leap in how humanity operates. A domino effect of sorts has occurred since a spark of innovation resulted in computers and the business application of computers. After tipping that first domino, a succession of walls surrounding the guarding of information (and by extension, knowledge) came down, and the benefit of this transparency is what humanity was seeking in order to evolve.

The availability of information drove more and more technology development. What started as a mechanism to make calculations to support conversations has morphed, seemingly overnight, into a mechanism upon which to have a conversation about calculations that should be made and how to make them. In this most profound paradox is a power source beyond what we can imagine even today and it is already unthinkable to consider conducting business without navigating both sides of this particular paradox of tooling how conversations occur.

So information technology, then, arose as response to a transformative event – a response that took root first in the Western Hemisphere and the population explosion of the post-World War II era. A western culture of do more, sell more, have more, and be more demanded IT and the development of IT led to an exploration of just how much more we could do, sell, have and be.

To say that information technology has affected every aspect of human existence is passé, but what is emerging from the innovation sandbox that has been referred to as IT up until now, is in fact a formation of pillars for human social, political, spiritual, and economic structure. Not only has Information Technology reshaped what we think of as possible and normal, it has exemplified and foreshadowed a way of life.

Practitioners in the computer technology world have built their careers in an environment founded in co-creation, dealing in the unknown, trial and error, group-genius, ingenuity and innovation, and exponential life-cycle maturation. These characteristics match the characteristics of the New Millennium business environment and serve as a lighted path of relevant competencies and experience for business to draw upon in moving its entire population into a transformational mindset.

So not only has what we refer to as 'tech culture' crossed over to become business culture in many ways, assumptions about information technology being a separate and incomprehensible thing are falling away. IT is becoming a comforting pal, like our car, the seat we always have on the bus, our television, or our daily newspaper. We love IT when we can rely on it and it works, we pound our fists when IT breaks down or malfunctions. IT makes or breaks our day – gets us in touch with each other and with the information we need to make the most of every minute of our lives and each opportunity that arises.

Industrial Age methods have been applied to the control and direction of information technology as a resource to business with limited effectiveness. This is because IT is at odds with the very nature of Industrial Age thinking. IT is all about human enablement – it is accessible and creatable on an individual level, regularly birthing new life-enhancing gadgets that save time and save lives. In turn this ease and fluidity sparks a question in the minds of employees about why their employer has not yet delivered IT to their desks at work in a way that has a real leveraging and lifting effect. Security controls, process controls, governance controls, and financial controls in turn need an IT solution to get them to synchronize and fade into the background so that day to day work can be elevated by IT... Yet another paradox to navigate.

One paradox that is unbalanced in many organizations is that Information Technology is being applied as unifying and empowering agent in an environment that highly values controls which separate people from each other and people from information. This is a fundamental reason why IT departments in these organizations cannot deliver on their share of corporate strategy and business plans. However, from automation to innovation, and from intelligence to connectedness IT is taking a new place as a great leveler in most businesses. IT spend is placing more emphasis on connecting people than on supporting processes.

CHAPTER SUMMARY

Navigate Paradoxes Tenet - Central Concepts
- Power is generated by identifying, assessing and navigating the paradoxes present in transformational environments.
- Resolution of paradoxes is a direct path to increasing Change Capability.
- Elimination of paradoxes is a direct path to increasing Change Capacity.
- Publicly Identifying and discussing paradoxes is a fast and effective way to anticipate ambivalence and avoid it.

Characteristics of the Transformational Organization
- Acknowledges the paradoxes present in the change activities and supports individuals and groups in navigating them. Knows that

wisdom can't surface when assumptions are dominant and unchallengeable.

As it Appears In Communication	As it Appears In Leadership
• Describes the high level paradoxes present in the transformational work that the corporation must navigate • Conversational tone is acceptance of the tearing effect of paradoxes while eliciting structured feedback • Synchronicity of communication is common	• Works to surface the paradoxes within the minds of individuals through conversation and listening • Addresses the paradoxes in a group setting by inviting ingenuity and innovation to creatively resolve the ways to navigate the paradoxes • Moves with the ebb and flow of contextual changes as paradoxes are 'surfed' into resolution

Embrace Error |

"Employees and organizations have reciprocal obligations and mutual commitments, both stated and implied, that define their relationship. Those agreements are what I call personal compacts, and corporate change initiatives, whether proactive or reactive, alter their terms. Unless managers define new terms and persuade employees to accept them, it is unrealistic for managers to expect employees fully to buy into changes that alter the status quo. As results all too often prove, disaffected employees will undermine their managers' credibility and well-designed plans. However, I have observed initiatives in which personal compacts were successfully revised to support major change—although the revision process was not necessarily explicit or deliberate. Moreover, I have identified three major dimensions shared by compacts in all companies. These common dimensions are formal, psychological, and social."

— Paul Strebel, Harvard Business Review 1996

Iterative processing is cheaper than ever and breaks transformative change down into digestible chunks. Other terms for this kind of approach are iterative development, incremental improvement, rapid development method, and agile method – but at their essence all of these follow a trial-and-error pattern.

Trial-and-error methods accept the fact that less is known going into the tactical planning of an initiative than is needed for success and they foreshorten analysis efforts aimed at turning unknowns into knowns. Less obviously, trial-and-error methods acknowledge that some part of the work will end up being tossed out as new information comes to light and new truths register at a deeper level with the professionals and executives responsible for the work. Iterative approaches have traditionally worked well for technology initiatives. They fit a profile where few facts are considered consistently true over the life of the project, and where so many unknowns are present that by the time fulsome analysis is completed the window of opportunity for change will have passed. And also, iterative approaches fit situations where: a great number of possible solutions are evident; where there is a high degree of complexity in the work; and where the risk to the organization is high.

Most major projects in the last 20 years have met these criteria and characteristics due to the complex nature and escalating pressures in business environments. That is, although projects were planned using Industrial Age sequential (e.g. waterfall) methods, they acted like trial-and-error incidentally due to their nature.

SEQUENTIAL METHOD

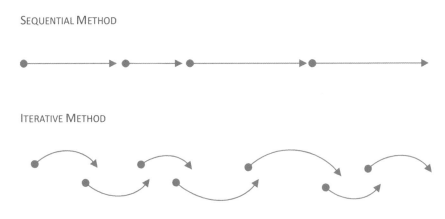

ITERATIVE METHOD

What has been troublesome about incidental trial-and-error is that the error part comes under the scrutiny of Industrial-Age-steeped leaders who judge it as 'failure' and the throw-away portions of error are judges as inefficient even by of Information-Age-aware leaders. These judgements manifest either directly in the initiatives shutting down before learnings can be harvested and the project has a chance to capitalize on them, or indirectly by 'shunning' the employees who were responsible for the work - regarding the project with embarrassment, or taking more serious actions. Shame is injected into the psyche of organisational change and this casts shadows that inhibit the 'try' portion of trial-and-error for years.

Since the acknowledgement and embracing of the 'error' part of trial-and-error has not be stated clearly in the psychological and interpersonal 'contract' between employees and the organization when the transformation work begins, staff are rarely acknowledged for their efforts to drive change through on projects or within operations. The work to grow and transform the company carries a stigma of shame that is magnified by lingering transactional leadership styles that favor reward and punishment techniques. In more broad terms, as stated in previous chapters, applying Industrial Age methods to transformational situations has the reverse effect on getting changes through as quickly and confidently as is possible.

Not only is 'error' misconstrued as failure, it is often thought of as a waste of time and money rather than valued as a part of the journey to enlightenment that is required for the organization to transform itself. It should be said that regardless of how well the organization supports transformational work, the trial-and-error cycle is very hard on the ego of the people involved, and so it is imperative that 'error' be embraced with an equal enthusiasm as 'trial'. Trial-and-error can be just as personally rewarding as command and control so long as everyone understands the ways in which the trial-and-error work is valued by the organization, and they understand the ways in which transformational change is achieved. Moreover, hiring organizations are more and more often quoting an ability to succeed in environments with a high degree of ambiguity though the support for doing so may not yet be robust. Having the ability to pull success out of the disarray after error occurs makes for a worthy performance metric and skill development target as a start.

Industrial Age methods are founded in sequenced, quantifiable pieces of work that add up to a greater-than-the sum-of-its-parts product, or service, or outcome. Few businesses can define their operation in these terms in the New Millennium. Most organizations are realizing that their success strategy is to make leaps in knowledge generation and leaps in ways of applying resources. Great leaps like these demand an injection of profound wisdom into the organization by any means possible. Some of this wisdom can be hired through consulting support, but the majority of it must be earned internally through the application of the minds of the organizations' employees in trial and error.

To open the way for learning from the chaos that can accompany 'error' each function within the organization must arrive at a moment of acknowledgment that hiring or acquiring the knowledge and wisdom required to make the jump to New Millennium light speed cannot be accomplished in great enough volumes to transform in time. Then, a percentage of staff must transcend the command and control they are accustomed to and work to provide anecdotal- or testimonial-based comfort level with trial-and-error amongst their peers.

Freed from the confines of the research and development department, trial and error offers daily new learning and leverages ingenuity, but only so long as the organization shifts its definition of individual performance and measurable work progress to intangibles like:

- regularly sparking ingenuity,
- speed of recovery from error,
- interpretation of results,
- nimble reinvestment of new learnings for greatest momentum ,
- identification of unexpected beneficial outcomes from trial-and-error work,
- capitalizing on the strengths of co-workers,
- ability to anticipate issues and opportunities in ambiguous circumstances, and
- ability to discern what matters from moment to moment.

NEGATIVE MOTIVATION

A popular North American management tactic has been to motivate through negative psychological methods such as competition, shame, withholding or delay of appreciation or reward, codependency, coercion, withholding of resources, judgement of performance rather than measurement of performance, reduction of channels for expression, shunning, dictatorship, fear-mongering, psychological manipulation … the list goes on. In some cases these tactics are taught, in others employees bring them into the workplace from their private lives. Most often these tactics are applied unconsciously - they are part of the fabric of our social systems and so deeply engrained that they have a life of their own.

Because indoctrination into negative psychological motivation began at birth for most people living today, we cannot be trusted to see precisely when we are applying them and when we are not – either to others or to ourselves. Studies have shown that negative motivation has short term effects and produces temporary results – which was perfect for assembly line and hierarchically structured business environments, but is largely ineffective in matrix managed organizations and especially the emerging 'New Millennium' social structure.

Negative motivation tactics are based in fear and as such can only create an emergency response or reaction to an event. With transformation becoming a way of being on a day to day basis, the level of stress caused by the fact that error is inevitable, and considered shameful can be so high as to push people to extreme behaviour. Some will go through the motions of co-creation and then scratch their heads and shrug when outcomes are poor, others will check-out on the job or switch jobs in search of a less stressful environment (that may not exist), and others will make superhuman efforts and suffer health problems. Anyone in business over the last 30 years has seen these kinds of responses escalate due to the friction caused by the incidents of 'error' produced as a natural consequence of the experimental nature of transformative change and the iron-fisted mental state resulting from fear of failure.

With negative motivation a larger and deeper part of the psyche of executive, management, and staff than we can see, it stands to reason that no amount of effort is too much in making the 'error' part of trial-and-error acceptable.

MAKING ERROR OK

To achieve the optimal mindset for New Millennium success when starting from a viewpoint muddied by the indoctrination of Industrial Age leadership and management methods requires a monumental shift from 'error is bad' to 'error is closer to success'. The former generates doubt and the latter generates courage. Furthermore, in the hesitation and loss of learnings brought about by feeling shame after trying and failing competitive advantage drains away as trillions of bits of data whiz through our society driving customer demand and new business contexts that the organization is now less equipped to keep pace with. By the time you have recovered from the emotion associated with Industrial Age perceptions of 'error' the opportunities have passed and the strategic objectives driving your organizations transformation may be obsolete. New Millennium business doesn't wait around for shame and disappointment, dismay and shock to pass. It just moves on without you.

If in a transformational world your organization is not experiencing failures you are not competitive. More to the point, if your organization is not experiencing failures it is not learning its way toward its next transformation quickly enough. From another perspective, the opportunities for success surfaced by the learning brought about by error are exactly what the money invested in transformational initiatives is for. Again, this is an opposite stance as compared with traditional Industrial Age thinking. Being on the edge in this way your organization is firmly in the stream of creating new business contexts and is mobilized to respond to changes in consumer demand.

So, making error ok in your organization is paramount. Some would say this effort is a cultural shift, but I believe the matter is much larger and more about moving external global culture inward. The organization internalizes the global shift in ok-ness of error as part of a movement toward self-acceptance, freedom of expression, and sharing rather than withholding appreciation. The world is becoming more and more fuelled on appreciation in fact. And in such an environment derision of those who have tried and erred has a dramatic slowing effect. Trial-and-error thinking and expressing things in terms of learning and appreciation iterations is a skillset that must be taught and measured like anything else. All levels of the organization must understand how trial-and-error behaves, and must be shown how to move with and through trial-and-error to continuously generate transformative momentum.

Thankfully, trial-and-error is a natural evolutionary process that, once set free, should gain momentum quickly. And, a huge upside to making error ok in your organization is a reduction in stress and unleashing of innovative thought – provided the efforts are serious and supported in ways that the average employee can see are legitimate. Sadly, an outcome of the straddling of obsolete command and control methods and structures and the connectedness and collaboration structures has resulted in a good deal of mistrust and loss of faith between employer and employee. Much thought should be given to how the embracing of 'error' is accomplished.

Rooting out the vestiges of ingrained negative perception of 'error' is a constant activity for the foreseeable future. We cannot possibly have the perspective to know how deep this negative thinking goes within the organization – it is an individual effort, made individually, and from one individual to another. Initially a great deal of pushback can be expected from those who have built their sense of self-esteem and professional success on the pillars of Industrial Age command and control and negative motivation of self and others. Staff at all levels will need to see both the support and encouragement of the acceptance of error and the erosion of negative motivation to adopt the new thinking.

The transformational organization embraces error as a valued component of the construction of the corporate knowledgebase. There is an emphasis on the value of experimental thinking and activity within the structure of corporate, divisional, and department strategic objectives.

An organization that embraces error rewards trying and failing with support mechanisms and funding for the capture of learnings, and future exploration and qualification of the new opportunities surfaced through the incorrect steps made, dead end paths taken, and miss-timed decisions. A prevalent feeling of 'whatever happens, we will figure it out' is a characteristic of the transformational organization and a thirst for knowledge is considered paramount among the personnel assigned to project work in particular.

As a way of bolstering morale through ambiguous and complex situations, bravery is identified and celebrated. An emphasis on what new pathways and alternatives sprung out of the failure is ever-present. Leadership is shared through a common awareness and acknowledgement of individual capabilities and the constant efforts to develop people through the work they are doing.

Leaders inspire new ways of looking at the situation: new ways to apply learnings; and the impetus to distill wisdom; they facilitate a discovery of what the effort and failure meant to individuals and group. The leader takes the initiative to communicate opportunities uncovered up the line and to interdependent work streams, functions and initiatives.

INFORMATION TECHNOLOGY AS THE MENTOR

A microcosm demonstrating the effects of shifting attitudes surrounding trial-and-error and 'error' specifically can be seen within the Information Technology function and now it has evolved over the last 30 years. Grass roots IT people have made a life's work of transformative change in broad terms and technology has been and continues to be both a trigger for transformative change and a servant to it.

In the early days everything IT was experimental and unpredictable. IT produced a significant percentage of the leverage opportunities during downsizing and flattening work during the 80s and 90s and became a go-to and seemingly bottomless well of solutions by senior managers during that time. As passionate and often self-made IT folks spurted possibility after possibility and ingenious solution after ingenious solution, management steeped in Industrial Age thinking had a hard time figuring out how to practically apply the concepts and tools IT was developing. As they started to see the influence of IT on their businesses from competitors and external sources, even the most ridged of thinkers began to look at IT as table-stakes for doing business at all at a minimum and a way to further business interests in all directions at a maximum. The problem they perceived was one of control.

Part of the problem of control had to do with applying dynamic, agility-producing solutions to ridged, mostly sequential and silo'd organizational structures, human resources frameworks, and operational practices. The other part of the problem was harnessing the products of ITs thoughts so that they may be understood and qualified according to the organizations goals and strategic outcomes. IT became a highly personal matter among senior business leaders – some saw IT as a way to promote their professional standing, others saw IT as a threat to their continued professional success. Both polarizing and connecting at the same time IT became a football in an organizational and personal identity crisis.

With IT budgets skyrocketing in the euphoria produced by at once seeing and resisting its potential, where to place IT in order to focus resources was a growing problem over the 80s and into the 90s. The solution most organizations arrived at was to rein IT in while organizational changes were made to receive the solutions IT was proposing. During this time IT landed in finance most often reporting to the CFO as a result of this tension. Through the pushing and pulling and as IT funding became more controlled and the organization worked to align IT with its strategic objectives, many brilliant IT people found themselves marginalized and having few channels for expression of ingenuity. Experimental scientists by nature, the IT leaders' expression of 'new things we can do' clashed with the creatively dry environment within Finance. Over and over IT was asked to demonstrate its value and produce justification of expenditures on its work. Unable to express this and being misunderstood by the CFO much of the time, IT languished in an underfunded state that persists today in many organizations. IT leaders led to their profession by a passion for innovation found themselves silenced and confined. The processes, procedures, and due diligence that served an assembly line mentality netted a set of good-governance practices for IT but also slowed the ability of IT to respond to business needs – in some cases nearly halting throughput of IT work. The numbers were now in balance but the agility, responsiveness and ingenuity that is typical of creative work had been lost. Moving into the New Millennium IT people saluted the flag on command and control methods but are rarely genuinely surprised that they don't produce expected results in throughput and agility.

Today, with massive complexity and variability, the average IT person is confronted with the task of applying command and control management to an erratic and unpredictable environment that is often in conflict with itself as it evolves to serve the organization. Thankfully the business side of the equation is catching up in its ability to understand the need and ways to be nimble in applying one wave of efficiency generating solutions after another and one wave of competitive advantage leveraging solutions after another. Software houses and tech companies served to preserve the tech culture over the 90s and through into the New Millennium. These organizations both set the pace for, and acted as an example of, the kind of agility and connectedness that underpins the emerging global socio-economic environment.

The shift in individual productivity and ingenuity brought about by personal computer and telecommunications devices and services (among many other factors) has reduced the average corporation's ability to influence its market from the inside outward and, in this new marketplace, the corporation must find ways to be the first to understand the nature of their consumers' needs in depth as they emerge and not in advance. For many organizations this is a complete reversal of thinking.

So eventually, IT has generated the transformative effect that it craved as it languished within Industrial Age-steeped organizations, and those organizations are beginning to reach out to their IT people for lessons in how to spark agility and ingenuity in its people and practices. Having adopted a fair chunk of Industrial Age thinking as a matter of survival and maturation, IT is often at a loss in responding to this change in attitude.

With a new sensibility - a transformation in thinking and in practices - money is once again being poured into IT. This time, the objective appears to be to get around the restrictions of command and control, essentially funding the following Industrial Age methods and practices while constructing Information Age (and beyond) methods and practices. Accomplishing this is the subject of much business transformation work.

Thankfully most IT functions are well rehearsed in straddling the two paradigms. As the CIO dukes it out with the other executives at the various governance tables, situation normal at the operating and project levels of IT is still very much trial and error, contingency, triaging, and individual ingenuity. The point here is that the business side of the equation finds itself in need of developing these capabilities, but appears to deny the fact. For example, we are all beginning to move in the Information Age way but are still measured in the Industrial Age way to a large extent.

In order to sustain and increase employee commitment under this particular stressor, Industrial Age tactics aimed at separation of people from each other and from information must be reversed – this includes dissolving the separators between IT and the business. Put another way, IT can teach business how to straddle the two paradigms, but to do so it must abandon Industrial Age methods. More to the point, what purpose is served by such an investment when a longer leap will catch the organization up with the New Millennium 'Age'.

CHAPTER SUMMARY

Embrace Error Tenet - Central Concepts
- Industrial Age separation from each other and from information must be reversed
- Manipulation (command and control) is a temporary motivator and has temporary results
- Patriarchal shame-based motivation is outmoded and adversely affects success for transformation initiatives
- Moving in the Information Age way and measuring performance in the Industrial Age way results in confusion and hinders the creativity needed to transform
- When error is an accepted part of trial-and-error Change Resiliency increases

- When error is an accepted part of trial-and-error, Change Immunity decreases
- Ambivalence is much less likely to manifest when 'error' is considered to be as important as 'trial'

Characteristics of the Transformational Organization

- An emphasis on the value of experimental thinking and activity. Rewards trying and failing with support and funding for capturing the learning's and exploring the new opportunities present in the errors made. A prevalent feeling of 'whatever happens, we will figure it out' is a characteristic of the Transformational organization. A thirst for knowledge is paramount.

As it Appears In Communication

- Celebration of bravery in the pursuit of transformation.
- Emphasis on what was learned and what new ideas sprung out of the failure
- Issues are not negative nor are they stressors
- Unknowns are not stressors but are opportunities

As it Appears In Leadership

- An conscious awareness of individual capabilities and need for development of people through the work they are doing
- Inspires a new way of looking at the situation to see new learning's and wisdom as well as opportunities
- Facilitates a discovery of what the effort and failure meant to individuals in a group setting
- Encourages the communication of opportunities uncovered up the line and to interdependent work streams and initiatives

Acknowledge Complexity and Scale |

"But whether the starting point is good performance or bad, in the more successful cases I have witnessed, an individual or a group always facilitates a frank discussion of potentially unpleasant facts: about new competition, shrinking margins, decreasing market share, flat earnings, a lack of revenue growth, or other relevant indices of a declining competitive position. Because there seems to be an almost universal human tendency to shoot the bearer of bad news, especially if the head of the organization is not a change champion, executives in these companies often rely on outsiders to bring unwanted information. Wall Street analysts, customers, and consultants can all be helpful in this regard. The purpose of all this activity, in the words of one former CEO of a large European company, is 'to make the status quo seem more dangerous than launching into the unknown.'"

– John P. Kotter, Harvard Business Review 1995

For decades we have been quoting the double-your-estimate rule of thumb for change initiatives, however in the case of transformative operation the time to complete transformative work is inestimable in practical terms due to a combination of complexity and volume of unknowns associated with the work. Most organizations will base staff communication plans on a foundation of strategic objectives and known factors, the latter being missing for the most part in major transformative efforts. At tables where the key messages of corporate announcements and circulars are formulated, transformations are described in terms of the strategic objectives, the business rationale, and process by which the changes will be undertaken.

Most often, this approach falls short in setting a useful expectation among employees. Moreover, the depth of complexity, breadth of scale, and the degree of the commitment required to accomplish transformation has been a point of denial among the leaders of the corporation responsible for communicating expectations. As strong messages from leaders have often been passed over in favor of flatly stated facts in corporate communication where transformation is concerned, the inclination to have outsiders deliver the 'reality' must be re-evaluated.

With the flattening of the organization having taken effect, most employees have been involved directly in projects leading up to or surrounding the core transformation that must occur, and are feeling the pressure of looming or ongoing transformation. Taking a minimization angle on messaging about transformation may be intended to avoid human ugliness. There is no sense trying to put a lighter spin on transformative change initiatives since the cat is well out of the bag. However, talking in denial of the scale and complexity of transformative change can spell disaster.

Still thinking they can *make* transformation happen, business leaders have been forcing transformation into a business change as usual template. However, transformational work cannot be treated as just another growth cycle, and conveying information about transformation in traditional ways by intention or naiveté amounts to dangerous understatement. People on all sides can see the permutations and combinations of interdependencies, and that transformational initiatives are casting off on a sea of unknowns. It is not that simply communicating the justification of the initiatives is inadequate, so much as this tactic incidentally telegraphs a frightful lack of acknowledgement of the magnitude and scale of transformation that is already evident at all levels.

So, making light of a transformative initiative or the probability that transformation is not a passing one-time effort compounds the gap between executive management and management and knowledge worker when it comes to implementing any change. Separation of any kind works against transformative efforts and therefore transformative change must begin with clear honest communication no matter how difficult the information is for staff to hear or for leaders to say. Communication about transformation should connect the people it affects and encourage each individual to assess the amount of energy and the level of commitment they would have to apply in order to fulfill their part in the transformative work.

PUSHING OFF POINTS FOR COMMUNICATING ABOUT TRANFORMATION

This book recommends that senior leaders begin to communicate an acknowledgement of the real and the inestimable scale of the demand that transformational work will place on people. Admit to the known complexity and monumental tasks to be navigated and also admit to how much of the equation of success cannot be known in advance. The following sections describe factors that add complexity to both daily operations and the matter of getting change through can be used as pushing off points in communicating an acknowledgement of the magnitude of work required to make transformation occur.

Starting With a Dirty Slate

It would be great if we were working with a clean slate as far as each functional unit being tooled, trained and resourced adequately. But in fact it's important to acknowledge that past changes may have been partially implemented, partially absorbed due to change saturation, or are just ill-fitting and badly designed. Doing so up front in general terms before examining the environment of each functional unit will help to suspend the 'you've got to be kidding' judgement long enough to establish dialogues.

Resistance is Futile and Everyone Knows it

Change saturation aside, transformative change goes well beyond what project-oriented Change Management practices can deal with.

Transformation is the new normal and is more involved than generating awareness and reducing resistance for this change or that change can accomplish. Shifting to transformational speed and resiliency is accomplished by motivating and leading differently for the long haul, and being clear about the permanence of transformational frequency and scale of change at all levels sets an appropriate expectation that individuals can make a personal interpretation about.

One thing is Certain, There Can be no Certainty

Much of what needs to change in the course of a transformational initiative is inestimable in practical terms. The amount of traditional analysis required to surface impacts, identify gaps and define requirements to build the critical mass of 'knowns' needed for refined planning and traditional directing of work would take an longer than the window for transformation typically allows. To admit this as a leader of transformation is to define a different way of designing, developing and implementing changes that people can understand and decide to embrace.

At a 30-thousand foot view it looks ok, but the intricacies of project and program interrelationships, dynamic teams and matrix management (to name a few) cross-cut the cost centre view in multiple dimensions. So much so that actually finding the person or people responsible for putting changes into operation and seeing them through is difficult to determine.

Not underestimating the complexity of the modern organization is a basis from which ballpark estimating the work required to execute transformational plans. Since so many unknowns are present when planning the work messaging any sort of confidence about budget and timeline is better not said. The truth is that we don't know how much it will cost, we don't know how long it will take, and we're not sure how it will affect you. What we do know is that it needed to be done yesterday, and a lot of ingenuity, reliance on peers, and connection of what is working with what isn't will be required.

Additionally, the responsible people might not be the people who have the knowledge required to get the job done, and they also might not be in a position of authority over those that do have that knowledge.

DOUBLE THE WORK

Operating in a transformative environment continuously means that operations staff must be ever adapting to a changing work environment. Naturally there will be peaks and valleys in the magnitude of the change the management and staff must accommodate and operationalize. There is no sense in minimizing this or allowing a perception that this might turn out not to be true to persist. In some ways transformative endeavors begin with the Acceptance step of the 5 stages of loss where change management ends. It capitalizes on the cold hard realization that something vastly different is being constructed that will demand a great deal from the people involved and also reshape how these same people work when the initiative is completed.

As management and staff build their future, it's better if they are acting in as full an awareness of the demands this will make as possible – furthermore as more and more transformative change arrives, they should settle into an operating model that allows and supports their ability to both operate and co-create a new environment simultaneously.

Denial of the additional demand on individual resources must be worked through on an individual basis. In some cases it will be one or more staff members drawing their manager through to a higher functioning state that enables the entire team to transcend the old paradigm.

The concept of redefining 'normal' will be discussed in greater detail in the chapter titled *Operate in Greyscale*, but for the purposes of this chapter, the fact that staff will be required to apply more of their personal abilities and aptitudes to nimbly operating in a constantly changing environment should be spelled out clearly in all communications. In bargaining unit environments this can be problematic but it is necessary.

When leadership practices and performance evaluations are aligned with transformational themes, the distracting friction between what is expected of people and what they are actually doing is minimized. Over and above this central point is the inevitability that one or more parts of the toolset and resources mix for any function or group will be ill-fitting, problematic, partially complete, or absent at any given time. This inevitability should not be overlooked or brushed aside. This should be acknowledged as the *new normal*.

THE GENUINELY SYNCHRONOUS FEEDBACK LOOP

None of the above described scenarios can successfully leverage transformative work unless a fully synchronous communication occurs that is a managed service conducted by a specific group. Here again abandonment of autocratic, or negative motivation tactics is absolutely critical. Pushing rationale for change at people does no good beyond setting a tone for organizational direction-setting. Its good but it doesn't reach far enough into the organization. In a scenario where making a connection between disparate pieces of information is everything, and trending can ferret out and surface issues with greater speed than direct one to one contact between people. A function-specific, trusted and consistent, two-way communication must be in place.

Individuals need to witness that they have been heard and they are going to be heard tomorrow and next week and next year to justify the level of commitment it takes for them to make the shift into a transformational organization. Traditional issues management and feedback collection, while valuable, are not enough and tend to slow progress and inhibit momentum.

Synchronous communication threads that are dialed up and dialed down in lock-step with the scale and frequency of change may begin with top-down communication but should ultimately end with change tactics being initiated from the functional teams or from individuals, bottom-up. I.e. the leadership kicks off the change and sets the direction, while the functional teams and key personnel take in what works and kick back what doesn't with ideas about what it would take to get the situation to work.

At the risk of going down the rabbit hole with this, the leaders at all levels of the organization where the tipping point is in applying more effort to get a change to fit and determine when efforts should be redirected sending the change back to the drawing board. What this means is that operations takes charge of the change much closer to design phase while they are also conducting everyday business.

With so much technology available to connect people in meaningful ways it is reasonable to think that, with some support and latitude, they could be used to trend and track ingenuity, measure connectedness and enable group genius as part of synchronous communications programs.

ASKING THE HARD QUESTIONS

Ultimately, transformation means turning corners and adapting to new priorities simultaneously across the organization – like a school of fish. All functions and personnel must not only be tuned in but already in motion. Maintaining an interested momentum among and between interconnected functions has a lot to do with asking questions. In such complex and highly work-loaded circumstances it takes a long time for the people impacted to become aware of planned changes and absorb them, though some people have a greater aptitude than others for this dynamic way of working.

As the investigation into impact winds its way through the organization, the people with the greatest knowledge are often the ones most pressured with work demands and so they may not participate to a level that ensures success. As the unfamiliar ways in which success is assessed under continuous transformation are discussed, a promise to ask and answer hard questions should be agreed in group settings. It should be made clear that asking question is the responsibility of each person even if the answer is "we don't know". In contrast to the usual impact assessment method, the discussion of impacts should focus as much on the impact of the new ways success is interpreted as on the impact of the transformation itself.

Discussed further in the next chapter titled *Build in the Breakdown*, creating a shift in the areas of the organization most steeped in Industrial Age methods and thinking or that may cling more strongly to the status quo requires compelling conversations and an injection of profound knowledge. Both of these are leveraged through the asking of hard questions starting with senior leaders. Here are some examples:

- What basic motivating factor is the company widely dedicated to?
- What long-term target or aspiration keeps the people in the organization engaged?
- How strongly do people identify with the image of the company?
- How is the way you are organized conducive to or a hindrance to success?
- How have innovation and disruptive technology played a role leading up to and in past attempts to transform?
- What systems and processes deliver an inherent competitive advantage to the company?
- How has the company determined and met a clear goal set previously? Are these tactics still working?
- Are current measurements leveraging transformative work?
- Has the company created significant differentiation in the market from a consumer engagement perspective?
- How have investment decisions been made up to the point of transformation and how will decisions be made in the future?
- Are programs and projects run with consistent efficiency and effectiveness? Is this a sufficiently strong capability within the organization to manage transformation?
- Does the company have a distinct advantage in process management?
- What special skills, abilities, and competencies are strongest in the company?
- Has the company maintained an advantage in scalability in response to market demands?

- Has the company identified one or more specific consumer outcomes to be optimized? Has it and delivered strongly on the brand promise to date?
- Does each individual in the organization know what made them successful? How do you know?
- What strengths does the company have that are becoming liabilities?
- What is the difference between your brand today and what you must make your brand stand for in the future?
- How must the core of the enterprise change?
- How must the context of the enterprise change?
- What fundamental capabilities must the organization acquire?
- In what way must the corporate culture change moving forward?
- How long will it take to remap the metrics that encourage the right actions?
- Have you made the entire investment in transformation or only part of it?
- What recognition, financial reward, or other personal satisfaction will individuals get for their efforts? Are the rewards worth it for the majority of staff?
- What are the real rules that determine who gets what in the company?
- Has your organization installed a tool or system in the absence of a process that utilizes the tool effectively?
- Does your organization suffer from solution overkill for the problem at hand?
- Do you have lots of data but no real information?
- Do you have a balanced and comprehensive decision-making system that goes beyond the obvious ROI criteria?

Questions should be aimed at linking the higher level concepts of how the organization plans to succeed on its new trajectory with the work occurring on the front lines and vice versa. Reframing the questions we ask each other away from 'risk' and 'return' (transactional) to 'purpose' and 'implications' (transformational) is a skill to be developed that enables synchronous feedback. Through this technique all minds are guided toward recognition of transformational cues that pull work through the complexity and ambiguity more effortlessly. That is, if you can formulate the right questions, clearer and more accurate answers will arrive that leverage efforts to transform.

Maintaining a synchronous connection in communication means that staff at all levels accept that they too must ask hard question of their managers. Asking questions prompts synchronicity and synchronization when answers are received however unwelcome they may be.

HEARING THE ANSWERS

Co-dependent Agreement is a psychological term used to describe situations in which people agree not to discuss a subject because it is too emotionally charged. Many organizations have co-dependent agreements in avoiding discussion of difficult realities. Although there are good reasons why nobody is motivated to come forward and take on the nasty job of intervening in this dysfunction, intervention is sorely needed, and transformation depends on it. Linking strategy to action is a huge step in creating the ability to transform, linking people in well intended honest discussion is a bigger step.

When no answers are forthcoming, or little is fed back to the person inquiring, there is no need for immediate alarm since the simple act of asking the right questions always yields a shift in thinking either consciously or unconsciously. Should there be little or no response over time, then a change in tactics is in order that assesses the reasons why no responses are forthcoming, and that elicits feedback in some form. Change management practices are most useful in these situations.

It is important to consider that answers to questions posed may come from many directions, and through a variety of channels, and the degree of dynamism in how each individual listens for and receives the answers is key to develop. Most communication is unspoken and often a shift in how we receive answers is as important to motivate as they nature and tone of how we ask each other questions.

SUPPORT BEYOND CHANGE MANAGEMENT

The formal practice of change management has been around for a couple of decades or more and was heretofore reserved for major projects that implemented business process reengineering or a new technology tool. However, change management has become a lifeline for organizations finding themselves in transformational circumstances.

Some business and technology leaders have taken up the Change Management opportunity, and made it part of their strategic toolkit. However, this can only go so far if a shift into a Transformational Organization Paradigm and is not also attempted. This shift effectively transcends change management and at the same time raises change management up to a new leverage point.

A stream of work that prepares the organization to lead transformation is required. This should be executed while at the same time developing change intelligence to open more room for change to occur. These two activities surround and lift heavy systems of control to avoid resistance building and alleviate the activity of removing barriers to change. Accomplishing this effectively makes full blown change management a feasible undertaking on large transformative projects and opens the pathway for change management to integrate into a daily activity. As staff participate in these new ways of working day to day they feel and interpret them as support offered along with the unflinching key messages surrounding complexity, scale and level of commitment required to transform.

OBSERVE THE WILDCARDS

> *"There is an obscure law of cybernetics—the law of requisite variety—that postulates that any system must encourage and incorporate variety internally if it is to cope with variety externally. This seems innocuous until you consider how variety shows up in organizations. Usually it takes the form of such behavior as siphoning off scarce resources from mainstream activities for back-channel experiments, disagreeing at meetings, and so forth. Almost*

all significant norm-breaking opinions or behavior in social systems are synonymous with conflict.

Paradoxically, most organizations suppress contention; many managers, among others, cannot stand to be confronted because they assume they should be "in charge." But control kills invention, learning, and commitment.

Conflict jump-starts the creative process. That is why the group process described earlier included a large number of stakeholders. When you extend participation to those really accountable for critical resources, or who hold entrenched positions, or who have been burned by past change attempts, you guarantee conflicts. But as the group faces and handles difficult issues, there is a shift in how they relate to contention. Participants learn to disagree without being disagreeable.

Emotions often accompany creative tension, and these emotions are not altogether pleasant. At Intel, conflict is blunt, at times brutal. Says one observer: 'If you're used to tennis, Intel plays rugby, and you walk away with a lot of bruises. They've created a company that takes direct, hard-hitting disagreement as a sign of fitness. You put it all behind you in the locker room, and it's forgotten by the scrimmage the next day.'

– Tracy Gross, Richard Pascale, and Anthony Athos, Harvard
Business Review on Change 1998

There is reciprocity of positive energy (not unlike a boomerang) available to transformative endeavors and the shift into a transformational organization through tapping into the work of the following groups and constructs.

- Information Technology
- Policy and Regulation
- In-house Counsel
- Human Resources

Traditionally work with these groups has been perceived more as obstructive to success than catalyzing. In part because they are perceived to be operating somewhat outside the hierarchical system (whether by design or in how their leaders are thinking) often these group are seen as unknowable quantities.

Relationships with these groups should closen rather than be distanced when approaching and executing transformation so that the reciprocation of transformative energy through conflict can be generated. That is to say, a repercussion can be expected from these groups when transformative change is afoot. Most obvious of these is information technology. IT is the group most sensitive to change regardless of how much they are pointed to as the initiator of transformative change.

Any shift in control systems, regulation, operational refinements, and organization structure has far reaching ripple effects in the IT realm which in turn ripple out to the rest of the company. In essence IT propagates the effects of change across the organization. It is the back door and short cut to all business functions and acts to condense the depth of recursion of transformative change so that all the interconnected levels of operating processes and informal activities affected must be dealt with more immediately. This effect magnifies the appearance of the speed of change and reveals the complexity of transformation all at once.

New insights are gained through the expression of risks and implications made by the groups mentioned above and the dissention this expression inevitably causes at discussion tables. These insights help connect the dots on how transformation should be achieved. Grappling to understand each other at discussion tables without applying co-creation and transformational leadership (i.e. by applying control-based and transactional methods) has routinely led transformation projects to failure. With the application of Transformational Organization Paradigm methods, apparent conflicts can yield a quick distillation of the fastest, safest, most effective path to the transformed state. In most cases this path is also the least comfortable one.

This concept applies at the individual level as well. The individuals that, under hierarchical, control-based systems, are considered to be renegades or wild-cards should be sought out and carefully tapped for new thinking in group settings. This is a tricky thing to do well, but can leverage the naturalization of transformational behaviour more widely as ideas and thoughts from these individuals are focussed on and proven to have value to the organizations change efforts.

A side benefit of tapping into friction points and renegade thinking is a naturally expanding belief among peers that although the changes are daunting in complexity and scale, they are possible to achieve. The price for not taking this approach becomes clearer and clearer as transformation efforts proceed. Transformation work starts on a downward spiral with the pulling back of people-energy. Do not shy away from difficult questions and highly charged differences of opinion. Not only is individual meaning and purpose revealed, personal investment is increased without strain. Each person is paid recognition and attention when fulsome expression of thoughts are made and the of habit half-measures is broken.

The transformation leaders most important tool when it comes to leveraging the wildcards and extracting ingenuity from disagreement is an uncompromising belief that success is possible regardless of the 'odds'.

CHAPTER SUMMARY

Acknowledge Complexity and Scale Tenet - Central Concepts
- Connect the dots on complexity.
- Connect with others to root out unknowns.
- Courage and bravery are common ingredients for success.
- The organization will get what it states as the vision and goal but the result won't look the way they originally thought it would.
- Not seeking perfection, seeking understanding is a key to success.

Characteristics of the Transformational Organization
- Telegraphs an appreciation of the adaptive agility groups and individuals must have to accomplish seemingly impossible feats. Builds on past successes and failures in approaching new large-scale transformations. A sense of adventure about embarking on far-reaching change. A prevalent feeling of 'whatever happens, we

will figure it out' is a characteristic of the Transformational organization.

As it Appears In Communication
- Clearly acknowledges the monumental challenges and seemingly impossible odds of success
- Uncompromising in its belief that success is possible regardless
- Clearly defines the characteristics and meaning of successful transformation
- Payment to staff is the attention to the complexity and recognition
- Expressing of thoughts beyond just communicating

As it Appears In Leadership
- Expresses business benefit in terms of meaning and purpose
- Holds to two or three unmovable constraints that frame the sandbox for creativity
- Does not shy from hard questions – says they don't know when they don't know
- Elicits courage and compassion
- Measures of the quality and results as well as the number of unknowns

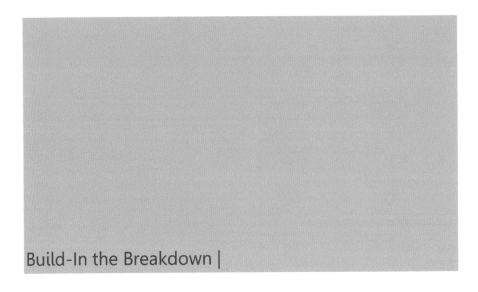

Build-In the Breakdown |

"When an organization sets out to reinvent itself, breakdowns should happen by design rather than by accident."

– Tracy Gross, Richard Pascale, and Anthony Athos, Harvard Business Review on Change 1998

As a leader in the transformational organization, factoring in the impacts of changes coming down the pipe toward your people is a much more frequent exercise. Particularly considering most managers and project leaders only periodically check-in on the progress of initiatives affecting their group. It's one thing for the leader to be engaged in the logistics of maneuvering change into the environment, it's another to engage staff in these activities as most of us know from past business process redesign activities. But, believe it or not, it will be necessary to pull your staff off the operations floor more of the time in order to fully shoulder the demands of the transformational organization.

Moving beyond wondering if this change or that will actually come to pass is a hallmark of the transformational leader. It doesn't matter if this or that change actually manifests, what matters is that your people are thinking about change at all times and never settling into thinking in absolutes. Movement is paramount in the New Millennium business environment and any kind of standing in sameness is a sign that not enough effort is being applied to what is on the horizon.

Acknowledging that the capacity of each employee convert change into business benefit varies, constant co-creation of changes and related transition logistics is a staple skill set for functional units within the transformational organization. Mobilizing a team that is in stasis is much harder than mobilizing a team that is already in motion. Once in motion, it is a matter of directing the energy of the group toward each objective as it emerges.

A previously unspoken truth lies in the notion of co-creating change and transition with the operations people… that is, it is the responsibility of the business unit to realize the stated benefits. This is a big shift from the old paradigm where the project team or change team was assigned responsibility for making sure benefits were realized. With co-creation rather than simple engagement occurring much farther up the chain in the product development or project management lifecycle, there can be no doubt about what the receiving operations team is expected to accomplish using the altered tools, processes and methods once they switch on the newly transformed state is flipped.

THE PERPETUAL TRANSITION PERIOD

In the continuously transformational organization the transition to operations in product development and project management processes begins at the design stage and is stated as such in the initiative collateral and agreements. That does not mean change management activities are sidelined, but it does mean that change management activities have a deeper and more meaningful interaction with the receiving operational team personnel and that they begin to deliver on risk mitigation and adoption strategy and much sooner. In fact, with more intense participation by the receiving operational groups, change management activities should be more natural and have better traction.

As operational co-creation of change becomes a mainstream activity, change management effort aligns more with Human Resources organizational development and professional development than with product, program, or project management. Human Resources functions can better support enterprise tools and practices in human inter-connectedness, evolve and deliver ongoing development and education in change intelligence skills, and can most readily integrate these into enterprise change management/leadership programs and practices.

The expectation that transformative change will be unceasing generates a number of shifts. Exception handling moves into a permanent business function and therefore matures. Pieces of management work that suffered from lack of attention despite best efforts, or thought of as too ethereal to grasp, crystalize into tangible and material elements of business lifecycles. An example of this is oversight of the 'concept' stage of the business initiative lifecycle which few organizations manage in a structured way unless they are in the research and development business at the time this book was written. As operations moves into the design, development, and implementation space, portfolio management activities extend farther upstream as well with senior leaders and 'excellence' oriented groups taking on responsibility for overseeing the innovation portion of business lifecycles.

The fodder for the innovation still comes from multiple sources, with one key difference: more innovative ideas arise from middle management and operations. Whether in response to stated transformational objectives, the marketplace as they perceive it, or longstanding misalignments in how work has been conducted, those with boots on the ground take a more fulsome role in creating transformation. The origination of innovation from these groups eases the work of managing change and enables the identification of breakdown points for structured and holistic breakdown/breakthrough management.

Furthermore, Change Management has a pivotal (although not new) role, in extracting and harvesting innovative ideas from the operational people using co-creation of transformative change methods. The Change Management function becomes responsible for facilitating the fully synchronous communication between staff and management, management and executive and between executive and management and management and staff on a day to day basis – leaning into operations to a greater extent much earlier in the initiative.

Not only is speed of transformation realization a critical capability to develop, generation, eliciting, harvesting, harnessing and managing transformative concepts, ideas and adaptations is the flip side of the coin of continuous transformation. The former cannot exist without the latter.

To be clear, what is being suggested here is that the operations team take on the design, development and implementation work associated with business change and transformation under the management of the project team and with support from process, organization, and information technology design and development experts. This represents an inversion of the definition of the subject matter expert with Change Management facilitating. Operations people are no longer subject matter experts to the product or project team. Rather they take a stewardship role and act as subject matter experts in the methods and practices for actuating transformation.

This approach has the potential to offer a great deal of job while it naturally builds, refreshes, and retains knowledge capital among permanent staff rather than project staff that move onto the next initiative. There is a natural and healthy alignment of responsibility and accountability for making transformation happen with the people who have the most 'skin in the game'.

Obviously making the shifts discussed above cannot be accomplished overnight, or without significant investment in developing middle management and operational staff in leading and managing structured transformation. However, with so much project work having occurred over the last two decades, few staff have not been exposed to the basic concepts required to lead projects. An added advantage is that the issues related to adequate engagement of impacted staff that have thwarted efforts to right-size and right-time change implementation would be greatly minimized. Greater efficiency and effectiveness in meeting the demands of the New Millennium business world is a natural outcome through pursuit of these shifts.

Interestingly, a case can be made for hiring permanent staff in headcounts matching those that are engaged as contract workers in this scenario. That is, much of the headcount represented by contract workers engaged on projects become operating functional unit staff with some number remaining contract workers engaged and funded by the functional unit to create flexibility in meeting highs and lows of transformation demand.

WHEN WHERE HOW of THE BREAKDOWN

Regardless of whether you apply co-creation methods or not, breakdowns in operations and in people can be anticipated over the lifespan of transformation. In fact if breakdowns are not occurring it is likely that the organization is not transforming.

A fundamental aspect of transformation is the marked break with the past, and if this is not felt as healthy tension, work disruption, or faltering on delivery at a few points in the transformation work, efforts to transform are not being maximized – they are costing more and taking longer to accomplish than is prudent, and the achievements made will most likely leave added work for the next transformative leap to accomplish.

At the strategy, planning, and phase review stages, where breakdowns are expected should be the subject of analysis work between business analysts, Change Managers, stakeholders and subject matter experts. The activity of having this dialogue acknowledges the inevitability of very uncomfortable situations that will need to be managed carefully so that all people are moved to break-through the prevailing mindsets, assumptions, or norms that inhibit forward motion.

A starting point for identifying breakdowns is to constructively discuss risks in terms of the paradoxes of doing things in the opposite way the organization has been to produce results within the initiative and to deliver the context to operate within in the transformed state. Of course there will be more obvious breaking points that threaten the organization's ability to continue to operate, and there will also be situations that are unexpected that result in breakdowns.

The objective work to document breakdown points is to bring into agreement the set of activities specific to each breakdown that would be applied to convert the breakdown into a breakthrough. This goes beyond classic risk mitigation to charge the breakdown experience with enough support to create a marked shift in thinking that is consistent with the new behaviors and characteristics present in the target transformed state.

It should also be said that the sooner the initiative and the organization gets to and moves through breakdowns the faster it will transform. This is an extremely powerful viewpoint to take so long as it is oriented as realism and support rather than oriented as just more mindless 'pushing'. Transparency is key to the success of identifying and managing transformation breakdowns.

Forward motion is always set in a context of the affirmative and not the negative in order for the transformational organization to move with and through breakdowns, converting them to breakthroughs.

FREEZE vs MATURE

This book is not in favor of using the word 'freeze' in any sense as it relates to iterating business change. What others may refer to as 'freeze' this book refers to as 'realize'.

What should be occurring is more of a leap frog effect where the recursive nature of incorporating change into standard procedure occurs in lock step with the iterations of implementation of change. There is a permanent staging area for the emerging and altered operations environment that is staffed by operations people who have been educated in business process design, transition management, change management and project management. What's 'in' and what's 'out' in this release of the business function is administered on a continuous transformation calendar or at an investment-risk or change-risk cut-off point that takes into consideration the specific circumstances affecting the ongoing success of the affected business functions. This is referred to as 'emergence'. Responsibility falls to the functional unit to bear the logistics responsibility for the timing of delivery of multiple interdependent projects. This is accomplished in full collaboration with all other functions affected by the projects.

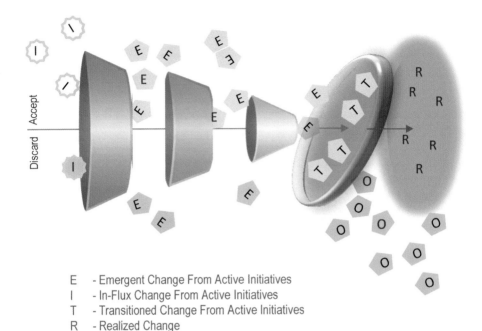

E   - Emergent Change From Active Initiatives
I   - In-Flux Change From Active Initiatives
T   - Transitioned Change From Active Initiatives
R   - Realized Change
O   - Obsolete Portions of the Operating Environment

An objective of continuous staging is that the changes which operations co-creates with the project or product team are more mature upon implementation. This does not mean that they are perfect but rather that they are fully functional and capable of generating a negotiated portion of the original business benefits. Taken to an extreme, this method produces recognition that the newly operationalized changes have a limited lifespan before they too move into entropy and are candidates for renewal and transformation. The accountability for maturing altered or transformed states as quickly as possible while capturing the benefits rests with operations and is considered job-one.

There can be no question in the minds of staff taking in each wave of change what they are supposed to do, no question what the benefits to their efficiency and effectiveness are, and no question what the company intends to yield as a result of their efforts. Like fashion, the operations environment is never 'finished' in the New Millennium. And confidence born from a sense that changes are mature tends to focus the efforts of operational people in executing the latest (temporary) processes, using the latest (evolving) toolset.

Within this knowledge the effects of the 'error' part of trial-and-error are highlighted. There can be no question that learnings from unsuccessful attempts are as or more important than learnings from successful attempts in generating positive outcomes in future transformations.

NON-AVOIDANCE of BREAKDOWN

All of the above sets the stage for a discussion about non-avoidance.

Industrial Age methods and thinking valued smoothness, elimination of conflict, constancy, and assimilation as keys to business success. In the New Millennium, the active pursuit of turbulence, breaking through long-standing paradigms, cultures, and ways of interacting is pivotal.

In fact, most resistance to any scale of change rests in the notion of condemnation (or fear of condemnation) for making mistakes. Resistance is also motivated by a fear of a loss of 'self' in assimilating into new norms. Assimilation has traditionally been part of the 'covenant' the individual makes with its employer. Furthermore, to not comply and conform, carries with it a punitive threat in some form whether spoken or inferred. So there is a tearing paradox here that sets the stage for breakdown identification.

Traditional practices involving 'indoctrination' no longer serve the organization and can hinder success over cyclical breaking down and reconstruction of the business over each and every serial transformation. As such the individual must be treated as an expert in their field and encouraged to have a sense of self outside their career and that work which they do within their employment contract. This approach recognizes and fosters the 'knowledge worker'. The portion of corporate belief system that is about 'serving' is what the worker participates in to drive a continuous connection with the needs of the consumer. Each team and individual identifies their value to the corporation and the value of the corporation to them with each successive transformation and as such can constructively break-down old paradigms and mechanics with their colleagues.

Most organizations will apply every resource possible to avoid breakdowns. In the process they also avoid the breakthroughs needed to transform. As some individuals will have a greater 'attachment' to the status quo than others, those that are able to foresee and qualify the breakdowns that may occur during any stage of transformative work must be engaged to assist others in dealing with the breakdown and moving through it in positive ways.

The longer breakdowns are avoided, the more costly the transformation and the greater the chance that the transformative window will be missed. That is to say, clinging to previous competencies and mindsets will be a hindrance, and conducting serial transformations is not enough to encourage teams and individuals to let go of them. There must be visible and apparent openings to latch onto emerging opportunities, and a trust that condemnation will not be a result of moving into and through breakdowns needed to transform. This concept goes beyond the 'forgiveness' of error – it reaches into and alters the psychology of how businesses operate.

Each person will react and respond differently to breakdowns. A simple measure to take in easing their passing, is to identify and communicate them broadly at the start of the initiative.

The transformational organization knows exactly where and when the old is disengaged and supports a suitable dis-engagement period encouraging the new paradigm to settle in and take shape at the same time. The transformational organization knows exactly where and when 'new' is engaged, it engages the 'new' cleanly with high morale and competency. A feeling of calm watchfulness pervades the journey to the transformed state, so that unforeseen breakdowns can be converted to breakthroughs. Transformation sponsors clearly identify which units or functions are expected to disengage from the old and the delta between when they were to have disengaged and when they are predicted to disengage. They clearly identify units or functions that are disengaged and in limbo and states when they are expected to re-engage in the new, transformed state. Transformation sponsors describe the work that can be done while in limbo state and describe the characteristics and reasons for early or late disengagement or re-engagement.

The leader of transformation knows the markers and characteristics of readiness for disengagement, and watches the arrival of the moment of disengagement with the group all the while inviting commentary from the individuals in the group. They acknowledge the limbo-state the group is in and create a sense of purpose within it. The leader of transformation checks and rechecks readiness with individuals and watches the arrival of the moment of re-engagement with the group, consistently inviting commentary from the individuals within the group.

HOW DO WE KNOW WE ARE TRANSFORMING?

Benefits realization measurement is only one part of the equation when it comes to determining whether or not the organization is achieving the target transformed state. The transformational organization is kenning its eye on the horizon to identify where the next transformative event will occur and where it will impact them while the last transformation is settling in, or more likely, is still underway. The next major jumping off point is ascertained by measuring the accomplishment of the bursts of transformation in hindsight.

To stay that real time intelligence about what the last or current transformation is yielding is essential is an understatement and this is something that is recognized as most companies work on developing Business Intelligence functions. However somewhere between Change Management and program/portfolio management a way to gather benefits measures made by operations and compare them with past and emerging transformative demand must be made. As operations inhales change demand and exhales ingenuity and innovative ideas, Change Management must capture and structure this new thought along with learnings made by the project and program teams. Ultimately Change

Management acts at all levels in their role as facilitator of synchronous communication and keeps the administrative middle ground between operations ingenuity and ideas and executive strategic innovative concepts.

Assisting in perpetuating the momentum of innovation and co-creation as the engine of transformation, the program/portfolio management function works to crystalize the potential of each initiative concept and make its potential application to meeting transformative demand clear. This is a new analysis role that precedes business case analysis. It is a joint effort between the strategic level of the Change Management function and the program/portfolio function. Some organizations have started down this path by striking a Business Transformation office that tries to combine the two functions. However, often the innovative concepts originate from the executive suite and are pushed down through to operations with little or no reciprocal communication or innovation dialogue.

It is important to note that the first transformative spark has to come from either the field or the executive suite but each successive transformation is fired by a synchronous exchange of thought. This exchange should follow the same disengage-shift-reengage pattern as operations does with the same approximate timing.

A simple way to measure whether you are transforming is to compare the inside to the outside of the organization to see how well the inner workings of the organization meet the characteristics of the New Millennium 'age'.

CHAPTER SUMMARY

Build In The Breakdowns Tenet - Central Concepts
- Breakdowns are identified during strategic planning for the transformation and at key points in the detailed planning of transformation initiatives, and their phases.
- The sooner breakdowns are encountered and converted to breakthroughs, the faster and more effective the transformation

is.

- Operations takes a much greater role in co-creating the transformation working with each project in much greater depth and sooner in the project lifecycle than for other kinds of projects.

Characteristics of the Transformational Organization

- A feeling of calm watchfulness pervades as the people and groups anticipate break-points that mark a successful transformation. Supports the people and groups going through anticipated or unexpected breakdowns, converting breakdowns into breakthroughs. A common knowledge that co-creation of transformation is key to reduce the disruption caused by breakdowns and breakthroughs.

As it Appears In Communication	As it Appears In Leadership
• Clearly identifies which units or functions are expected to break with the past and the nature of the breaks expected • Clearly identifies units or functions that are working to breakthrough • Identifies the support network for groups, individuals, and functions approaching or emerging from breakdown	• Accepts breakdown as a natural part of transforming and a good sign that transformation is occurring • Applies transformational leadership techniques to leverage conversion of breakdowns to breakthroughs • Marks the entry points and exit points to and from 'breakdown' and celebrates successful conversion of breakdowns to breakthroughs

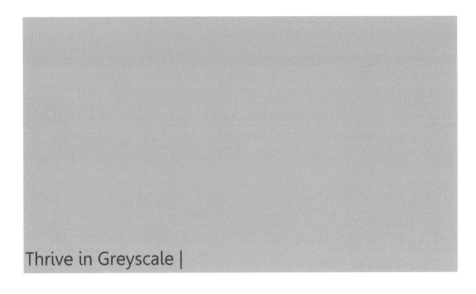

Thrive in Greyscale |

"When a company sets out on the journey of reinvention, it must uncover and then alter the invisible assumptions and premises on which its decisions and actions are based. This organization context is the sum of the past and dictates what is possible for the future. When managers reinvent themselves and their companies, they create a new context that leads everyone to embrace a seemingly impossible future."

— Tracy Gross, Richard Pascale, and Anthony Athos, Harvard
Business Review on Change 1998

Thinking of business in absolutes or black-and-white terms although entrenched in most business paradigms and some professional disciplines is dangerous at the best of times and this concept is amplified in the New Millennium. With transformational change occurring month to month what was fact last week is most likely fiction this week and so an untethered feeling accompanies ones approach to the day's work.

In previous socio-economic and cultural norms, trust was thought to be fostered by a sense of certainty, an expression of unshaking confidence by leaders. Under these paradigms hierarchical structures flourished. With more humanist thought germinating in the 1960s, these structures and their underlying assumptions have come under increasing scrutiny. The main force of the question being 'is this good for people?. As masses of everyday people gained access to higher education and generally elevating their level of awareness through the 1980s and 1990s the stage was set for a critical mass of shifts in direction setting, power, and wealth from a 'few' to 'many'.

A law of nature is that growth and ongoing elevation must occur else entropy take hold and with this in mind an evolutionary leap of the 'humanist' attitude could be anticipated and expected. Less well understood or discernible in pre-millennium decades is the escalating speed and complexity of day to day business and living. Technology both mitigates and enables that speed and complexity. As business leaders begin look to IT to help them understand the intricate inter-relationships between functions and structures of the business. IT is less capable of seeing the human aspects of why the business moves and operates as it does having been groomed to be a fundamentally utilitarian. The ability to understand the complex inner workings of the average organization, in order to predict and manage the impacts of transformative change, is not held within one or even a few senior people. It is held in pockets across the organization, and in the nebulousness of relationships between people and teams.

A natural tendency to cling to ridged and absolute attitudes, assumptions, and ways of interacting (receiving and sending knowledge) varies in its orientation and severity from person to person. In some cases the tendency borders on an addiction or emotional aberration, in other cases the tendency is expressed as a preference or position for the protection of the individual or team. Herein lays the work of the Change Management professional in aligning the varying mindsets of people and equipping them to lead through change.

However, the assumption of the Change Management activity is that a plateauing or settling in period will be possible between major changes and this is not the case in the New Millennium business environment. In order to build the capability of the organization to adapt with greater speed, frequency, breadth and depth, it's people must become better at operating in 'grey' and must abandon the long-held attitudes and assumptions of black-and-white thinking.

While some organizations have been doing lip service to the arrival of a heightened state and deeper depth of change activity and a growing fog of ambiguity surrounding day to day operational success, few have taken action to prepare their people for it. Nor did they make sufficient adjustments in their process controls, practices and methods to accommodate it. Operating in 'grey' is so foreign a concept that most organizations were stumped as to how and when to move next.

In basic terms, operating in 'greyscale' means that the organization is in flux at any given time, from its cornerstone core values, through its definition of identity, its perception of success, its governing bodies and protocols, its processes and procedures, the skills and abilities it values and seeks in its people, and the way in which is selects and wields its tools. What was true and right yesterday may not be true and right today or later in the week. Good judgement is replaced by constant re-assessment and the ability to see beyond the horizon and select pathways of activity that serve the twists and turns in direction and objectives - an exercise in visioning and re-visioning.

The forming truth can only be discerned by honest and open discourse among knowledgeable people. Once discerned, courses of action can only be formed on partial information and can only be activated through a common commitment to making routine leaps of faith. Not only is transformational leadership key in the ability to operate in greyscale, the ability of all staff to release their attachment to 'norms' is equally critical. Guiding the application of effort in this context is a large piece of work.

There are discrete skills required to be successful operating in changing shades of grey and these can be developed. These skills surround the following descriptions:

1. Without some structure, it will be harder and harder for your staff to tell what is true or deserving of their attention and what is not. As changes materialize into the operating environment a real danger is present in people spending effort as well as attention on the wrong things.
2. Building a tolerance for unknowns and seeing them as acceptable and non-threatening maintains the kind of judgement and

perspective required to notice opportunities and issues arising and make adjustments or clearly carve off items unworthy of attention in favor of spending time and energy on those that hold more promise and payback.

3. Approximating the goal and interpretation of sketchy work objectives is a collaborative effort and the practice of co-creation should be applied.

What people are thinking about, paying attention to and then applying their energy and effort to is a judgement continuum akin to playing a space-wars game where the player tracks oncoming crafts and judges when move, when to shoot, and what order to shoot in for the highest score. The objective is to level-up in the game effortlessly, at the right time for your organization, and with the right intention where your consumers are concerned.

DEFINING A NEW NORMAL

In transformational environments standard approaches no longer apply. It may be hard to accept, but conducting thorough analysis of requirements before design and development is next to impossible to do. Managing projects in waterfall style is not feasible. Two-stage operations engagement (design and transition) leaves too much margin for missing the mark. Amassing knowledge within the project team then teaching it to operational staff at deployment time is too much knowledge to transfer in one go.

The above standard approaches are replaced with the following in a transformational organization that thrives in greyscale.

1. Characterize the target altered environment and allow the business function to define and redefine detailed design until transition time.
2. Iteratively develop the altered environment accepting the extra cost of a certain percentage of throw-away work.

3.   Co-create (over design and build phases) the current iteration with equal participation by the functional units. Put operations in charge of identifying what part of each iteration is the throw-away part and what is net new in the next iteration.
4.   Build in an amount of recursion that keeps the business running, throw away everything else that is 'old'.
5.   The project provides the structure for the work then guides operations in completing the interpretation of the changes and developing them.
6.   The emphasis of work is on where the organization is going and what state should be achieved, and less effort is made to examine the particulars of the current state. Thought capital is expended on how to build something completely new again and again rather than how to adapt the old to meet a new set of requirements.
7.   Operations is responsible for reporting against benefits realization targets at straw model stage, and again at transition stage.

A new normal surrounding the control of transformational work includes an acknowledgement of: the uncertainty about how much it will cost; the uncertainty about the scale and scope of work to be conducted; and the uncertainty of just what the impacts will be. These uncertainties are a function of the complexity of modern business and one more set of uncertainties can be added to the list that pushes the entire perception of how the work might get done off any kind of bearing : Uncertainty about who is accountable; uncertainty about who is responsible; uncertainty about who is leading at any given time. An up-front assumption should be made and internalized: the transformed organization will be nothing like the current organization, each evolution will yield an organization that is completely new in every regard and will demand a complete release of the old organization in order to be successful.

Due to the ascension of the transformational organization most companies have found themselves perpetually 'in project'. Conflicting priorities among project and non-project work change day today and can be sweeping in nature and that often means work is let go of when it is half completed, being considered no longer important or relevant. This is disconcerting and disappointing under the Industrial Age paradigm, but is considered a building block under the Transformational Organization Paradigm.

The transformational organization purposefully manages changing influences and new realizations that can only be gained by moving through transformations – it translates these into day to day priorities and measures success differently than in the past. People are not measured by traditional measures of achievement in a transformational organization. And more importantly, the environment people are working in is productive and has less waste because one piece of work creates a basis of learning for the next that is harvested among operations employees.

What this means is that the rejection of changes is at the discretion of the line manager. They control the efficiency factor and are not imposed upon to accept half-baked change. Because they and their people co-created the changes, they can be very specific about what exactly needs refinement or correction in order for the change to be acceptable within the context of the benefits they are expected to realize.

Hand-offs are smooth and contingency plans don't linger. The line manager is not by passed but instead 100% empowered to co-create the change and then also reserve the right to alter the change after weighing the trade-offs. This kind of empowerment demands that the line manager is highly connected with their peers and the interrelated functions elsewhere in the organization – capable of negotiating with those individuals and capable of knowing the right time to cut off development for this 'round' of change and adjusting operations to accommodate.

As solutions change mid-stream, project and operations staff change mid-stream and design specs are altered by new circumstances and pressures after development has been completed. Along with the co-creators, line managers implement small changes that have integrity immediately and understand what is being let go of and what is being kept, cutting off lingering wish lists.

The leaders of transformation hold people together and go with what works right now, since it inevitably reflects strategy right now, and the immediate demands the company is attempting to address.

Experimentation will be needed often and so task force teams are a key element to trying out risky solutions in favor of gathering needed information and reduce unknowns. Time-boxing is recommended.

A new normal in the transformational organisation is that people move without hesitation to pat down new change and immediately carve off any 'throw away' work produced during the iteration assigning it to a learnings archive. Decision making is democratised in this way and energy is reserved for the next transformative change coming down the pipe.

New terminology springs up to describe uncertainty and working in shades of grey, and these show up in internal communication. Trending current thought is a feedback mechanism to the executive in determining whether or not they are transforming. Employees mobilize and stay mobilized reaching for growth opportunities personally and for directing the right mix of their own personal skills and resources to the work of continuous transformation. Job hopping is commonplace and serves to disperse newly developed capability around the organization. Energy flows freely directed by ingenuity and democratised decision making. Success is measured by the amount of new knowledge and insight gained in each iterative implementation.

Executives actively gauge the repercussions of the initiation of a transformative change – small movement at their end of the transformational setting, means large movement at the opposite end and this is a focus of what the executive is measuring at all times.

There are still many and balanced opportunities to be the hero in the new normal. There are numerous and balanced opportunities to feel the satisfaction of a new definition of 'completion' and deep understanding of subject matter – possibly in new and even deeper ways - to be very competent in the midst of the sea of unknowns. The joy of the workplace is found in 'the making' of the workplace which is in the hands of the employees of the organization like never before. Leaders are demonstrative in their participation and add the final context for 'completion' and the assimilation of learnings.

Fulfillment from growth has always eclipsed fulfillment from stability or financial abundance throughout mankind's history. This fact underpins the reversal of thought that characterises the New Millennium; the inversion of attitudes and the focus of activities to prosper within it, and the prevailing belief that growth and stability are mutually exclusive states. That is... in the New Millennium, the pursuit of individual growth and fulfillment at all levels manifests in stability and financial abundance for staff, the organization and its consumers.

In the transformational organization, the investment in the pursuit of the unknown delivers the knowledge required to succeed. Attitudes that are black-and-white are considered divisive and as representing a risk to the wellbeing of the company.

DECIDING WHAT IS IMPORTANT

"Have a Road Map Even When There Are No Roads"

– Norman R. Augustine, Harvard Business
Review on Change 1998

Acuity is not the only determinant of what is most important. In fact firefighting is a huge temptation for most organizations as they approach the scale and complexity of transformation with command and control methods in hand.

Where selecting and tracking initiative progress and business value is concerned, a formula for transformative value of initiatives should fit within the program/portfolio management function. The assignment of transformative value is work that should be conducted among the executive with the assistance strategic Change Management and operations management and staff.

But what about transformational work underway?

This is where analysis effort should be applied. A less structured and more interpretive aspect of business analysis is applied when changes in priority occur and when each plateau of new information is reached. The new work of the Business Analyst is to ask:

- What pieces are irrelevant?
- What pieces of information have meaning?
- What speculation has a ring of truth?
- What harsh realities should be taken very seriously and which ones are actually passing from view as the transformative environment emerges?

WHEN TO IGNITE COMMAND AND CONTROL

A technique that has been used with success over the past years is to carve out well defined work packages and execute them. This holds true in the transformational organization with the caveat that any number of truths can emerge, as less well-defined pieces of work proceed, that can impact what has been completed. Rework is a large part of both iterative approaches and the Transformational Organization Paradigm and should be thought of as an opportunity to fine tune solutions to better meet changing transformation demands.

As a rule of thumb, switch to command and control and transactional leadership style as soon as a piece of work is well defined or else when 70% of unknowns are known. Symptoms of the 70% threshold being met are:

- Requirements analysis is no longer being conducted formally or informally.
- Fits and gaps have been identified and enough is known that solid gap filling or sidelining can occur.
- Inspirational approaches are getting old and are no longer well received .
- The change management team has a level of confidence that training can be developed and delivered in a complete and cohesive way.

- The transition pathway is clear even though roadblocks and barriers exist.
- Feedback from line managers and teams estimates that 70% or more of the change implications and information is present.

When ascertaining whether or not the organization is making progress on transformation, measure the percentage of unknown at each iteration or checkpoint, measure public opinion, measure personal investment and commitment of staff and contractors, measure whether the characteristics of the target are close or far, measure the confidence among management and staff of their ability to get new solutions to work or finding new solutions.

Rather than focus on issues and issue resolution, focus on known/unknown ratio and focus on workability confidence. Move forward in the affirmative and discard the negative.

CHAPTER SUMMARY

Thrive in Greyscale Tenet - Central Concepts
- In-depth analysis to turn unknowns into knows too slow for transformation to be successful.
- Ingenuity and innovation are paramount even though they appear to foster even more unknowns.
- Bring all minds to bear to co-create the future each step of the way.
- Things appear to be going faster when there are more unknowns but this is not necessarily the case.
- Multi-disciplinary skills among staff can be developed quickly when navigating the sea of unknowns associated with transformation.

Characteristics of the Transformational Organization
- A prevalent feeling of 'whatever happens, we will figure it out' exists across the organization. Celebrates autonomy and the change intelligence of the organization and its people. Harnesses group genius at all levels and applies it to the quest for converting unknowns to knowns. Harvests the emergent knowns at the right time to convert to operational change and benefits realization.

Unknowns no matter the size or scale are considered acceptable and reasons for mobilization rather than shutting down.

As it Appears In Communication	As it Appears In Leadership
<ul><li>Describes what is needed in terms of characteristics rather than specifics</li><li>Identifies key unknowns to resolve as king-pins for forward motion</li><li>Confirms and reconfirms constraints as a framework for creativity</li></ul>	<ul><li>Enables autonomy</li><li>Sees when to mobilize based on unknowns becoming knowns</li><li>Prepares the characteristics of mobilization – critical mass of knowns - with the group to define go-time</li><li>Discourages black and white thinking and attitudes</li></ul>

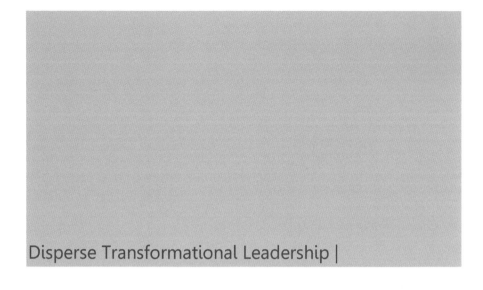

Disperse Transformational Leadership |

"…we Westerners have few mental hooks or even words for excursions into being. The Japanese chart the journey across life in terms of perfecting one's inner nature, or being… In contrast, Westerners typically assess their progression through adulthood in terms of personal wealth or levels of accomplishments. To the Japanese, merely doing these things is meaningless unless one is able to become deeper and wiser along the way.

Many Western CEOs will undoubtedly say that all this smacks of something philosophical or, far worse, theological and therefore has presumably little relevance for managers. But an organization's being determines its context, its possibilities. Remarkable shifts in context can happen only when there is a shift in being."

— Tracy Gross, Richard Pascale, and Anthony Athos,
Harvard Business Review 1993

As most businesses sit poised on the precipice of truly participative leadership and organizational models, looking over a vista of possibilities on the other side of a wall we have been scaling this past decade, many are wondering if they have the courage to make the remainder of the journey.

So much chatter has gone on around the matter of enabling workers to be self-directed and interchangeable – knowledgeable and capable of executing the responsibilities and taking on the accountabilities of multiple roles with little preparation. However there is limited capability to absorb technology tools that enable learning at lightening speeds, and that enable moving 'socially' primarily among the Post-Depression Era, Baby Boomer, and X generations. The importance of sharing or dispersing leadership has been mentioned in previous chapters as a key ingredient to successful transformation. Like any other way of working in the New Millennium, a measure of synchronicity is required for any activity to produce results. Since many people in these three demographic groups are in leadership seats they must take initiative to demonstrate the interchangeability they desire of their people.

DEMOGRAPHICS – ERAS AND AGES

Currently, most organizations are facing a 5-tiered generational demographic among its employees from executive to field operations. This presents a communication gap of epic proportions under the New Millennium context. Leaders face an unprecedented challenge in bridging the gap to maintain the common understandings that underpin the strategy, and a unified identity, culture, and value system. Motivation to invest personally to the depth required for in transformation takes on a daunting profile whether from the motivator or motivatee's perspective.

X-Gen personnel have had the luxury of a unique, non-committal viewpoint situated between *Baby-Boomers* still steeped in traditional ways of succeeding hanging on from turn-of-the-century Industrial Age mindset, and the *Y-Gen*-ers that form the leading edge of the 'Millennials' are scratching away at Industrial Age assumptions. When you juxtapose the *Millennium-Baby* existentialist and abundance-oriented value system against the aging Post-Depression Era shortage and servitude value system, there is a LOT going on.

X-Gen personnel are best positioned to reconcile all perspectives, mitigate resistance points and create common ground. They are uniquely positioned to lead *Y-Gen* and *Millennium-Baby* staff toward strategic objectives, have an ability to translate *Baby-Boomer* and *Depression-Era* directives into language and meaning that *Y-Gen* and *Millennium-Baby* people can absorb.   Conversely *X-Gen'ers* are able to turn around and express Y-Gen and Millennium-Baby innovation in terms *Baby-Boomers* and *Depression-Era* people can absorb.

Age and Generation Alignments

Industrial Age	Industrial Age	Information Age	Millennium Age
Post-Depression	Baby Boomers X-Generation	X-Generation Y-Generation	Y-Generation Millennials

That said, the emphasis of effort to integrate the sensibilities of all 5 generations should be focussed on the younger generations in order to capitalize on all they can do, all they can take in, and all they want to offer to businesses and organizations. They embody the values of the New Millennium 'age' and have the best viewpoint from which to turn the organization onto the new trajectory. While we can expect the older generations to continue to heavily influence supply and demand on all fronts, it is the younger generations that hold the better part of innovative potential.

Never before has a demographic group had such a clear view of their own self-worth. Whether an outcome of women's emancipation, the children's rights movement, or the effects of the Information Age, the *Y-Gen* and *Millennium-Baby* generations have it more or less together and don't accept the same old lines about teamwork and performance and doing what is asked of them without question. As a generalization, they know no fear – that is to say they are not governed by fear and cannot be motivated by Industrial Age notions of what 'respect' is. 'Millennials' are more 'evolved' in their thinking; they know they have as much to offer as anyone else; they have a base of global economic, philosophic, social, and technological knowledge thus-far unprecedented in human history; they look to apply themselves to some fulfilling and meaningful purpose and living happy lives; they tend not to ask for permission, and they expect fair compensation that has nothing to do with 'reward'.

'Millennials' have an intrinsic sense for creating and know the feeling and amorphous process of co-creating something with peers and acting freely on ideas. They are the first generations to have the means and channels to manifest their ideas into concrete products and combine those products with others around the globe, evolving and maturing them rapidly into something material, consumable, valuable, and in-demand. They are able to create demand without first creating a problem to be solved. Much of what the 'Millennials' are doing is based in taking up the existing capacity that is unused due to ridged processes and converting it into a business.

I needn't quote examples of Uber, Facebook, the creator of Spanx, the Kardashians' franchise etc. to make my point. 'Millennials' able to create socially responsible enterprises are the next leaders of our world – and businesses are at a point where they can achieve great gains by adapting structures, policies, cultures, methods and practices to match the way in which the *Y-Gen* and *Millennium-Baby* generations work. In large part, transformation is the way in which we are preparing our world for the 'Millennials'.

Look to *X-Gen* people to bridge the gap between and among the following polarized concepts...

Values Translation

POST-DEPRESSION BABY BOOMER	Y-GENERATION MILLENNIALS
Conformity and Sameness as Belonging	Diversity and Acceptance as Belonging
Mass Consumption Equals Wealth	Niche Customization Equals Wealth
Fear of Poverty and Loss	Trust in the Variety of Abundance
Milk Current Opportunities	Reach for New Opportunities
Follow Authority and Question with Care	Follow Value and Offer New Perspectives
Uphold the Status Quo	Disrupt the Status Quo

Motivation

POST-DEPRESSION BABY BOOMER	Y-GENERATION MILLENNIALS
Command and Control	Inform and Inspire
Separate People From Each Other	Connect People In New Ways
Separate People From Information	Stream Information Along Multiple Channels
Message Shortage and Competition	Message Valued Contribution and Experiential Learning
Give and Take	Share
What it Means to the Boss and the Company	What it Means to the Employee and Consumer

Without significant effort on generational integration, transformation will be stymied.

EVERYONE IS A LEADER

Adequately tooled and informed, the *Y-Gen* and 'Millennials' generations are capable of taking on great volumes of information and converting it into leadership/motivation. With the need for supervision and management oversight shrinking and the breadth of knowledge the knowledge-worker amasses expanding, decision-making can shift from higher paid managers to knowledge-workers.

Combining the accountability and authority to lead others, with the information and knowledge to accomplish objectives, sums to a breadth and depth of work that is satisfying and personally rewarding. The average person is inspired and inspires others in turn toward the challenge the organization has tasked them with. Each person in the team leads all the others upward and onward toward the stated objective by expressing their individual talents, capabilities, skills and knowledge. Additionally, each team leads the organization as a whole to see new possibilities emerging from the combination of minds and tools applied to the work.

If staff are to weigh in often in terms of lending their knowledge to the transformation of the organization, and are expected to display ingenuity and be innovative at the same time, it is necessary that they are also leaders. In fact is quite impossible for staff to be innovative, knowledge contributors without also being leaders and having leadership skills.

ALLOWING AND REWARDING INGENUITY

Leeway to be creative and innovative in how one is doing their job or producing the defined results, generates a happy and highly engaged staff that will be sufficiently committed to see the result of their work through to full knowledge transfer and benefits realization. With a basic understanding about how transformation occurs and the freedom to adapt to change in their own way, the up and coming workers of the New Millennium are able to deliver the speed of transformation that the organization needs over the next 30 years.

With the diminishing of the Industrial Age methods, the fear about making a mistake, or transgressing some un-see-able cultural boundary, or missing a financial incentive by not following rigidly defined success behaviors goes diminishes also. A great releasing of much needed human potential follows.

WHY BOTHER

Executives of the organization are usually the hardest group to shift into New Millennium mindsets. No amount of training in change management is going to produce more success in transforming their business domain. The 5 stages of grief and the 5 stages of change are good to know about, but apply much less in the New Millennium way of doing business because they are fear-based responses to change.   That is to say: by the time the target transformed state is achieved, 4 of the 5 stages of loss and change will be minimized as fear is removed from the equation. Conversely, in order to transform, the leaders should be focussed on making this elimination of fear a reality while transformation work progresses.

128

In essence, under a continuous transformation paradigm executives and managers are routinely asking staff and each other to make a leap of faith – which is a different thing entirely from asking people to adapt to another change. The leap of faith is referred to as such for a number of reasons: many unknowns, demand for speed, immediate demand to make a greater personal investment. And, because the *ask* is a leap of faith, a removal of the possibility of a fear-based response is essential. Command and control or carrot and stick leadership styles are ineffective anyway and inspirational leadership styles characterised as Transformational Leadership are needed.

Few people do transformational leadership really well and there is a danger that inspiration comes across as hollow, has no credibility or is too wishy-washy to be trusted. Faith cannot be cultivated under a feeling of insincerity, so formal training in Transformational Leadership techniques accompanied by coaching support to embed the new behaviours is the minimum development work to undertake.

WHAT IS TRANSFORMATIONAL LEADERSHIP ANYWAY?

A number of schools of thought developed over the 20th and 21st century that describe leadership styles – particularly for business purposes. In examining these a clear correlation between Transactional Leadership style and Industrial Age command and control and between Transformational Leadership style and New Millennium 'Age' and connectedness and co-creation exists that cannot be ignored.

Command and control naturally flows from transactional reward and punishment activities where connectedness and co-creation naturally flow from transformational inspiration and individualized meaning.

For the record Bernard M Bass's definition of Transformational Leadership is...

Transformational leaders inspire, energize and intellectually stimulate their employees. They generate awareness and acceptance of the purposes and mission of the group, and they stir their employees to look beyond their own self-interest for the good of the group.

By comparison, to Transformational Leadership, Transactional Leadership is a less evolved capability, that appeals to basic needs (Maslow) rather than the elevated needs of people - as described on Wikipedia at the time of writing:

"Within the context of Maslow's hierarchy of needs, transactional leadership works at the basic levels of need satisfaction, where transactional leaders focus on the lower levels of the hierarchy. Transactional leaders use an exchange model, with rewards being given for good work or positive outcomes. Conversely, people with this leadership style also can punish poor work or negative outcomes, until the problem is corrected. One way that transactional leadership focuses on lower level needs is by stressing specific task performance. Transactional leaders are effective in getting specific tasks completed by managing each portion individually.

Transactional leaders are concerned with processes rather than forward-thinking ideas. These types of leaders focus on contingent reward (also known as contingent positive reinforcement) or contingent penalization (also known as contingent negative reinforcement). Contingent rewards (such as praise) are given when the set goals are accomplished on-time, ahead of time, or to keep subordinates working at a good pace at different times throughout completion. Contingent punishments (such as suspensions) are given when performance quality or quantity falls below production standards or goals and tasks are not met at all. Often, contingent punishments are handed down on a management-by-exception basis, in which the exception is something going wrong. Within management-by-exception, there are active and passive routes. Active management-by-exception means that the leader continually looks at each subordinate's performance and makes changes to the subordinate's work to make corrections throughout the process. Passive management-by-exception leaders wait for issues to come up before fixing the problems.

Transactional leaders use reward and punishments to gain compliance from their followers. They are extrinsic motivators that bring minimal compliance from followers. They accept goals, structure, and the culture of the existing organization. Transactional leaders tend to be directive and action-oriented.

Transactional leaders are willing to work within existing systems and negotiate to attain goals of the organization. They tend to think inside the box when solving problems. Transactional leadership is primarily passive. The behaviors most associated with this type of leadership are establishing the criteria for rewarding followers and maintaining the status quo.

Within transactional leadership, there are two factors, contingent reward and management-by-exception. Contingent reward provides rewards for effort and recognizes good performance. Management-by-exception maintains the status quo, intervenes when subordinates do not meet acceptable performance levels, and initiates corrective action to improve performance. "

When the prevalent leadership style falls within the definition of Transactional Leadership, an enormous challenge to success is presented to the organization undertaking transformation. A first step should be addressing the shortage of Transformational Leadership capability among the leaders charged with the accountability and responsibility for accomplishing transformation.

It is entirely possible to teach those who favor transactional leadership the techniques associated with transformational leadership. And the sooner this is underway, the better in terms of matching organizational leadership capability with New Millennium methods and the Transformational Organization Paradigm. These are intimately intertwined and it is safe to say that continuous transformation cannot succeed under a pervasive transactional leadership style.

To move from transactional leadership style to transformational leadership style requires:

1. Leaving behind motivating by *contingent reward* and motivates by *inspiration and intellectual stimulation.*

   Rather than promising a reward for good performance or application of effort the transformational leader embraces their responsibility for nurturing and supporting their staff. They communicate high expectations, use reframing and metaphor to focus efforts, convey important purposes in simple ways, and promote intelligence, and studied problem solving.

2. Leaving behind *management by exception* and actively *considers the individual* and holds attention through *charisma and influence.*

   Rather than setting the rules for desired behaviour then watching for and taking corrective action when deviations occur, the transformational leader mentors, coaches and advises their employees according to their unique abilities, talents and values. They deliver the vision and sense of mission among their staff, instilling pride of association, respect and trust.

The goal of the leader in applying Transformational Leadership techniques is to…

- Inspire with vision and individualized meaning
- Nurture intelligence and opposing points of view
- Extract direction from circumstances and experiences
- Allow for people-development in the midst of shifting ground
- Connect in a meaningful way with others
- Create and environment for two-way expression and acceptance of thought
- Pull change through into realization with the active cooperation of all affected
- Cultivate mutual acceptance of thought

In the New Millennium 'Age' the ability of the leader to motivate others to make a leap of faith with them into the unknown is a particular and skillset required for transformational initiatives to be achieved.

So, why is this particular set of skills and sensibilities so important in the New Millennium 'age'?

The answer lies in the compression and intensity of changes that are taking place as we round the sharpest corner of the pattern of evolution...

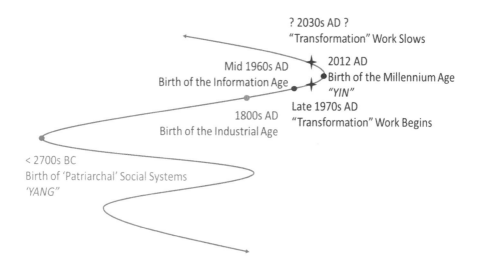

The new way of being is marked by a different way of measuring success, and how products are valued and consumed. This is so different from what we have known that the properties of this new way of being cannot be perceived in large part until experienced. We can only understand the characteristics at each juncture and learning point along the way to the transformed New Millennium state. And, as with regular change, each and every person involved in the transformation must themselves transform in order for goals to be achieved. This is a tall order.

Thankfully, unlike Transactional Leadership, Transformational Leadership does not require the person leading to have any particular level of authority. That is, Transactional Leaders should have the authority to deal out rewards and sanctions, carry and wield both carrot and stick; but Transformational Leaders need only have a voice at the table in order to provide leadership. In this simple fact lies the opportunity to spread out as broad a leadership capability as the breadth of transformational work demands.

Additionally, Transformational Leadership has the ability to universally motivate all generations present in the average workplace, though Post-Depression Era and Baby Boomers may struggle with the esoteric nature of its application.

VISION AND THE CONCEPT OF ALL-NESS

A good deal has been written about the value of having leaders with vision - those who can see the blot on the horizon and recognize it as the next major turning point. This book proposes that the average leader need not be such a visionary, but must be able to use a manner of divination to organize what is known into a general direction. And, above all, match the breadth of that direction to the breadth of efforts made to move forward along it. That is, a traditional approach to a linear, and two-dimensional set of efforts should be broadened to include all avenues of pursuit – at least for a period of time.

This is a concept referred to as all-ness.

So, in addition to the depth of reach the transformation leader achieves by individualizing their communication, motivation by appreciation, exploration of impacts, and demonstration of relationships, a second dimension of outreach is necessary. The transformation leader brings to bear all disciplines in equal amounts (HR, IT, BA, LD, Financial, OD&D, Governance, Operations, Innovation etc.) such that each discipline explores the new path, at the knowledge worker level, and educates the other disciplines in their findings and perspectives.

The transformation leader has the task of congealing the new information and perspectives into forward moving stepping stones. They also discern when new information has produced as much momentum as it can and a new set of learnings is needed.

Moving all aspects of a piece of work along at the same time is a tough sell, particularly to Finance who would prefer to see measurable gains for money invested in a more granularly defined way. Unfortunately, this method is too flat to yield the real progress toward the transformed organization after an initial burst of energy – typically the selection of a new technology toolset or governing framework. In the longer term, less is gained for the investment than might have been, or the investment originally projected creeps to higher and higher costs.

Moreover, traditional approaches tend to avoid confronting the hard issues, and tough questions and playing it safe has the reverse of the intended effect on risk management. I.e. the risks of not transforming fast enough are discounted and pursuit of reduction of opportunity costs is considered an unaffordable luxury. In fact the reverse is true, the real risk that is so difficult to embrace is that a dramatic loss can be realized by hesitation and the application of traditional risk management methods. This inversion of the notion of 'risk' is consistent with the general 'inversion' or re-polarization that is demanded by transformational work.

DATA FILLING THE GROWING DIVIDE BETWEEN STAFF AND MANAGEMENT

Executives cannot make necessary decisions or direct work without the impact of subject matter experts among their management and staff. In some cases they must reach through middle management to harvest knowledge from among their knowledge workers.

Each of executives and staff are polarized in their motivations and moving farther away from each other due to the pressure of constant and dictated change, resulting change fatigue and increasing reluctance and therefore capacity for more change. Executives need more and more from staff and staff have less and less to give.

IT has been filling the widening gap between executive and staff with data that offers a detached (unemotional) context between them. As executive, management, and staff all reach for answers, that pool of data falls short in supplying the intrinsic value that moves them enough to make a leap of faith.

Change in our still largely hierarchical command and control, carrot and large stick organizations elicits much emotion about the personal investment each individual makes in their career and for their employers. For executives what is at risk is mostly about their standing among their peers and their ability to move between organizations and maintain their professional value. For staff what is at risk is mostly about their ability to support their families and further the wellbeing of their children and care for elders.

Now that everyone is looking to the masses of available data for reasons to keep investing personally, they are realizing the data is a mess and this has raised the profile of the Data and Information Management discipline in most companies over and above what consumer demand has influenced alone. When leadership is dispersed as a way to leverage transformation success, this problem is amplified.

A DEEPER LOOK AT THE SHIFT

Regardless of demographic group, most of the current workforce is steeped in Industrial Age methods. As alluded to earlier in this book, the indoctrination of command and control goes back hundreds if not thousands of years – so it's safe to say that we probably don't even know when we are doing it and when we are subject to it.

A simple and effective way of breaking the habit of command and control is to choose a more 'transformational' response when faced with behaviours and events. Some to practice on are listed below:

- Ambivalence prompts Motivational Interviewing response
- Ambivalence prompts surfacing belief discrepancies coaching response

- Resistance prompts empathy response
- Barriers prompt opportunity talk and meaning talk response
- Change talk prompts values dialogue response
- Commitment talk prompts support inquiry and delivery response
- Denial prompts dispassionate display of relevant facts response
- Anger/Angst prompts silence response
- Bargaining out of change prompts information gathering and ingenuity response
- Acceptance prompts support inquiry response

ROLE OF THE LINE MANAGER

"Achieving this critical balance means managing the conversation between the people leading the change effort and those who are expected to implement the new strategies; creating an organizational context in which change can occur; and managing emotional connections, which have traditionally been banned from the workplace but are essential for a successful transformation."

– Daniel Duck, Harvard Business Review on Change 1998

The line managers role is a confluence of management, administration and leadership where the line manager is not the only person their direct reports take leadership direction from.

In a transformational environment the line managers role can be ambiguous or in some cases lost entirely. For the sake of completing the picture of transformational leadership within the transformational organization, the following is a list of activities the line manager still conducts whether they are in a transformation leadership role or not.

- Keep staff informed
- Select task force members for investigation of unknowns
- Manage logistics, balancing change development and stable operations

- Change intelligence measurer and coach
- Change intelligence behaviour correction
- Local leadership for all change
- Gate keeper for change
- Peer leadership measurer and coach
- Balancer of doing and thinking and creating
- Liaison with transformation leaders
- Break addictions to the status quo

CHAPTER SUMMARY

Dispersing Transformational Leadership Tenet - Central Concepts
- Innovation and co-creation demand dispersed leadership.
- Transactional styles of leadership are ineffective in transformational circumstances and are difficult to disperse without heavy hierarchies and process.
- Transformational leadership techniques support the nature of transformation work and can be dispersed and shifted from person to person.
- Where the individuals that make up the organization are concerned, the following are the foundations for their participation in any model:
  - What people know   -Knowledge
  - What people can do   -Ability
  - Whether or not people bring their best game -Intention

Characteristics of the Transformational Organization
- Leadership is rewarded based on its ability to harness human thought and convert it to business results or new opportunities rather than protect the status quo. Measures success according to the depth of synchronous communication and participation that takes place and the regular completion of the communication loop. Tends toward a think-tank mentality. Shift leadership from person to person depending on who has the most needed knowledge and skills in the moment.

As it Appears In Communication	As it Appears In Leadership
• Wording is centred on thought and ideas • Language is rooted in	• Motivates through defining the meaning and purpose of work at an individual

transformative terms and
phraseology
- Confirms that leadership by
each individual is critical

level
- Congeals the sum of parts
from all individuals into the
greater whole

Move Forward in Leaps of Faith |

"During our 35 years of research, writing, teaching, and consulting for U.S., European, and Japanese corporations, we have found, particularly in senior executives, an unwillingness to think rigorously and patiently about themselves or their ideas. We often find senior executives perched like a threatened aristocracy, entitled, aloof, and sensing doom. Flurries of restructuring or downsizing are like the desperate attempts of uncomprehending heirs who try to slow the decline of the family estate. Each successive reaction is misconstrued as bold action to "set things right."

When leading an organization into the future, executives come to a fork in the road. As they come face-to-face with their organizations' needs to reinvent themselves, many executives hope for the best and opt for the prudent path of change. Even when they choose reinvention, their feet get cold. Thrown into the unfamiliar territory of reinvention, where the steps along the path and the outcomes themselves are often unpredictable, the responsible thing to do, many executives think, is to get things back on track. It is not surprising that so many senior executives decline invitations to reinvent themselves and their companies. It is like aging:

experts tell us that it is difficult, yet most of us hope to go through it without pain."

– Tracy Gross, Richard Pascale, and Anthony Athos,
Harvard Business Review 1993

In the transformational organization, leaders not only direct the efforts of their people toward strategic goals, they harness the thoughts of their people and use them to propel each transformation forward. In the New Millennium business environment the leader is less often the hero and the team or group being led is the source of the ingenuity required to not only get transformative change to work, but they are also required to extract the business benefits before the conditions for this dissipate.

The necessity for motivating leaps of faith arises primarily from the volume of unknowns associated with the transformational work (as discussed in a previous chapter) and secondarily from the constantly changing conditions for success. Transformative change generally arrives in a wave over wave pattern. This is true for transformative events triggered by global business climate changes as well as for the execution of transformative initiatives that respond to the triggers.

The deadly nature of ambivalence and how to deal with it has been a subject of this book. The flip side, or other end of the continuum of human response to transformative change, is making a leap of faith.

The 5 stages of change as originally described by psychologist James O. Prochaska relates to a change in behavior that is deeply rooted. In relation to the subject of this book: switching ones approach from Industrial Age command and control to New Millennium 'Age' connectedness and co-creation. Where transformation is concerned, the stages have to do with moving from a state that is approaching obsolescence (on a downward spiral) into a state that presents innovation (on an upward spiral). Furthermore, in order for transformation to hit the mark, the jumping-off point from one transformation to the next must occur *before* the downward spiral begins. In this context, the leap of faith takes on new meaning. That is, leaps of faith must take place for transformation efforts to launch at the right time, then leaps of faith must take place for transformation to progress, and then leaps of faith must take place for transformation to be realized *before* the next jumping off point is visible on the horizon.

This concept is nothing new – typically describing the cycle of corporate growth and the strategically optimal time to move onto the successive cycles of growth. The point I am making here is that the 'right time' to jump into the next cycle is not based in research, historical trends, and empirical evidence where transformation is concerned, most of the information about the next 'cycle' (in the case of transformation 'cycle' equates to 'trajectory') will be discovered through the process of transforming rather than being known up front. As such making leaps of faith at all levels, over and over again to *create* the future state are needed.

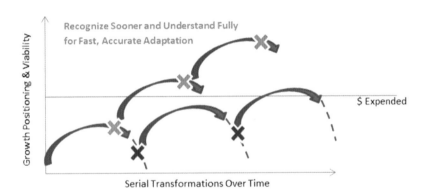

FOCUSSING OF EFFORT

The 5 stages of loss as defined by can be more closely associated with continuous transformation. While we each move between Industrial Age and Information Age and on through to New Millennium 'Age' continuous transformation is, well, continuing. There is no holding back the waves of transformation that are arriving with increasing frequency trying to contain them or push them back using Industrial Age control-oriented methods. Doing so only makes for greater and greater turbulence and ineffectiveness. Moving with and through those waves in adapting to transformative events is less painful and more productive but requires all organizational resources to be mobilized and remain mobilized.

Making a leaps of faith focusses the intention and attention of the individual or group. A heightened state of awareness and mental muscle is brought to bear on the work at hand, and historical, political and other barriers to progress are reduced.

When talking about committing ones effort through wave after wave of transformative change, managing the movement of people through the 5 stages of change, and the 5 stages of loss is necessary and global best practices in Change Management deal with this. However, time is a big risk factor when mobilizing transformative effort and maintaining it to achieve transformative progress. Enculturating, recognizing, and supporting, leaps of faith, especially at the operations level, makes transformation progress more predictable and consistent, even though this seems at first glance to be an oxymoron.

In other words, there is less and less room for moving through the 5 stages of loss associated with departing operational contexts, tools, rules, or truths with each successive transformation. And, there is correspondingly little time for the executive and management leaders to amass a set of knowns about the transformation work (up front or in a proactive way while work progresses) and then transfer them to staff in order to speed people through the 5 stages of change. All staff at all levels must feel confident they will be supported if they make a leap of faith with each new set of realities that are presented by transformational work.

Furthermore, the timing of the organizations adaptive response to transformative events is critical because many of the triggers of the events have a cumulative nature. In other words, wave over wave of transformation must be addressed – none may be by-passed or skipped - in order to have a longevity of business success in the New Millennium. The weight of this notion increases when we consider that a critical mass of the benefits of executing organizational transformation to meet New

Millennium demands must be achieved in order to be positioned for the next wave of transformation. It's not enough to go through the motions of adaptation without the follow-through, and this work in particular demands an enormous amount of dedication that only a leap of faith mindset can generate.

BYPASSING THE FIVE STAGES OF CHANGE AND GRIEF

Looking at this in more depth, an outcome of applying robust transformational leadership pervasively is that the denial, anger, depression and much of the bargaining stages of loss associated with departing operational contexts and success criteria are often eliminated in favor of a leap directly to acceptance of the emerging changes. Most transformational organizations will find that their operations groups spend at least 50% of their time and effort in the current operational context with 50% of time and effort spent in co-creating the emergent operational context. Correspondingly, the pre-contemplation, contemplation (earmarked by ambivalence) stages of change are much shortened under the Transformational Organization Paradigm. In essence the individuals co-creating the emerging operational context are making the leap into the future by-passing pre-contemplation and contemplation and also simultaneously working through those two stages as they co-create the new operational environment. These individuals are also communicating the reality of change to their co-workers. As the co-workers contemplate the coming changes they are executing the departing operational context. With change occurring on a more frequent cycle and operational group members rotating between executing and co-creating aspects of the business function, settling into the current operational context doesn't result in demobilization the way it does today. Staff are still in a heightened state, mobilized for change at all times.

As change cycles through the group, the line managers are challenged to keep everything on track and focussed. They must be effective in the current /departing operational context and be effective in the emerging operational context as they support their staff. Of all operational staff, line managers must be constantly switching contexts between current and future.

Not all people will be capable of making a leap of faith again and again and like any other era, leaders and managers must still utilize their people according to their strengths while developing them to every extent possible.

So, the objective here is not to have everyone make leaps of faith, but rather to have more and more people able to make leaps of faith. The more staff that are comfortable with this mode of working, the easier change will be for everyone else. This is because any ambivalence among the members of the functional/operations group becomes exceedingly obvious and can be approached with empathy and open conversation. Combined with a mechanism for the operational leader to reject co-created change based on supporting evidence and information, the operational function is empowered greatly in right-timing the transition and implementation of wave after wave of transformation.

Regardless, there is as much for Change Management to do, though their role at the operations level is more advising and supporting than educating. The important and significant thing to notice is that executing a more pure and robust Change Management discipline becomes feasible under the Transformational Organization Paradigm. Individuals and teams recognize most readily that they need Change Management support and meet the Change Management team half-way, rather than Change Management having to close the entire distance between the project team and the operations team (for example) as is often the case currently.

FAITH, TRUST AND DOING WHAT MATTERS

> *"Let me see if I can summarize the lesson: acknowledge the tragic pattern of corporate crisis; reverse engineer the steering mechanisms; subject the assumptions of the enacted strategy, especially market data, to measurable tests; open a strategic dialogue within the company; aspire to the freedom and discipline of scientists; redefine competitive advantage; develop measures to*

plot progress toward victory and a new strategic language to describe it… You cannot change an organization without courage, and you cannot induce courage from above, not even by example. What you can do, though, is make goals and methods transparent enough that your employees will be willing to take some calculated risks. You want hundreds of people making informed choices and taking timely action. You do not want them all second-guessing each other or wondering if the boss really means what he or she says."

– Roger L. Martin, Harvard Business Review 1993

The leap of faith can reduce paradox resolution work to some degree, as well as having a levelling effect on the need for developing Change Intelligence. That is, motivating leaps of faith is a top-down and lateral activity that increases Change Resiliency and Change Capacity. Additionally, it is impossible to motivate a leap of faith using Transactional Leadership techniques. Therefore there is a high correlation between the dispersion and embedding of Transformational Leadership and the ability of the organization to make leaps of faith that propel transformational work forward at the right pace.

A major tool to use in navigating the sea of unknowns, the leap of faith is helpful when line of sight is not possible. That is, moving in faith and trust that the individual and those they are working with will find the right solutions as work progresses becomes the norm when there is insufficient information or context to see the path forward.

Not only is the individual putting faith in the leader, they are putting faith in their own abilities and they are putting faith in the organization accepting and making use of their abilities. The individual is moving ahead in faith that they will not regret committing their greatest strengths to the transformative work only to have that effort produce more learnings than measurable progress.

What is powerful about the leap of faith is the emotional ingredient that can be referred to as 'hope'. Channelling emotional energy requires a leaders skilled in transformation techniques and who is genuine and compassionate at all times.

146

Part and parcel of making a leap of faith is an understanding that the individual is doing work that matters – it matters a great deal to the organization and everyone they work with. As the individual looks within for the courage to make a leap of faith they think about the 'self' first, followed by consideration of people and circumstances outside themselves, then (and this is the line of thought that triggers a leap of faith), they consider the greater good. If the organizations leaders cannot move their people into a mindset of 'greater than self', a leap of faith into the unknown cannot be accomplished.

Much change management work is conducted to move people's thought centricity from 'self' to 'outside of self' to 'greater than self' to gain commitment and reduce resistance to change. When the leap of faith is commonly understood to be well supported by the organization, more Change Management work can be focussed on steering the surge in energy generated by the leaps of faith toward productivity, results, and benefits realization.

Of course in order for the leap of faith to work, the demonstrated and clearly understood support from the organization must be exercised with the faith individuals have in their teammates. This is much different than having trust in teammates – which is a more tactical and less evolved version of the kind of maturity we are talking about here. Faith exceeds the need for demonstrated congruency and predictability. With the work environment landscape changing dramatically and often without warning, trust between people takes a back seat to having faith in others rising to challenges, in their own ways, which may appear to be untrustworthy.

Furthermore, what matters in one moment in time, may have no bearing next week or next month. Faith in others centres around a belief that they will do what matters most, which is discerned through combination of the unique strengths and abilities the person brings to the work, and the current and emerging definition of success. Great leaps in learning occur in witnessing others rise to challenges and overcome them using their unique set of strengths and abilities - learning that the organization can harvest and build upon with each successive transformation.

Not only is a leap of faith a movement forward, it is also done to leap from one set of understandings and context to the next as unknowns become knowns. New realities encountered demand dramatic changes in direction toward an altered position of success.

While it seems exhausting to make leap of faith after leap of faith, the reality is that because of the absence (or lower level of) fear, work and forward motion take less effort and produces less stress and strain than working under threats posed by command and control and reward and punishment methods. Fear of not achieving the reward can be as strong as the fear of 'punitive' responses when high risk, radical change work is undertaken. Not only does courage play a part, but for transformation to occur, courage must be shared. That is, one person displaying courage is insufficient to get the job done. Again, the Change Management role can more easily do its job when obstacles of duplicity, mistrust or confusion are reduced.

SAY GOODBYE TO THE STRUGGLE FOR LEADERSHIP

Leadership in a leap of faith environment must be dispersed and shared to create the amount of support needed. Otherwise the impetus for the work being undertaken is too weak. Leadership in a healthy leap of faith environment is unifying and not divisive – each person's strengths naturally 'take the lead' at the right times over the course of transformative work.

Struggles for leadership typically arise from disappointment or fear entering into the equation. In making a leap of faith each individual knows they can't afford divisiveness of any kind because all minds are needed, all viewpoints need to be expressed, and it is imperative that all thoughts and ideas are actively connected. This is much more difficult than it sounds and take, enormous effort to ensure.

THINGS TO MEASURE TO TELL IF IT IS TIME FOR A LEAP OF FAITH

The kinds of measurements discussed in this section are thumbnail in nature – more of a professional assessment (not unlike the change management concept of measuring 'readiness') than a metric.

Measurements to take to determine whether it is time to motivate a leap of faith include:

Measurement	Interpretation
Percentage of unknowns	The higher the percentage of unknowns the greater the need for leaps of faith.
Personal investment and commitment	Discern the difference between resting and withdrawing. Withdrawal signals a need for motivating a leap of faith.
Whether the characteristics of the target are close or far	When the organization is perceived to be far from 'being' the New Millennium characteristics a leap of faith is indicated.
The relative turbulence of the environment	If the work environment, targets, and conditions of success are changing radically or rapidly or both (increasing or decreasing) a leap of faith should be motivated.
The confidence among management and staff of their ability to get new solutions to work	When people are becoming disappointed, moving into doubt or fear-talk or there is a sense of 'hitting a wall' a leap of faith should be motivated.

In doing these assessment style measurements, make every effort not to fall into expressing things as issues. Focus on known-unknown ratio, focus on workability, confidence, and changes in energy.

CHAPTER SUMMARY

Move Forward in Leaps of Faith Tenet - Central Concepts
- Support leaps of faith among a critical mass – not everyone needs

to make a leap of faith.
- Leaps of faith provide clarity and encourage commitment and innovation.
- Working in the future not the past is necessary for transformation to occur – a leap of faith generates forward momentum as the past is released more readily.
- Doing what matters most right now in the current context before the context changes generates speed, where hesitation results in constant context switching without much progress.

Characteristics of the Transformational Organization
- Leadership is rewarded based on its ability to harness human thought capital and build momentum. Faith and trust in the capabilities of oneself and one's peers is commonplace and forms a basis of individualized motivation and teamwork. Fear-talk is absent, replaced by critical thinking and strategy.

As it Appears In Communication	As it Appears In Leadership
• Wording is centred on affirmative activity • Language is rooted in transformative terms and phraseology • Confirms that leadership by each individual is critical to success • Confirms that the unique contribution of individuals is critical to success	• Motivates leaps of faith over and over again based in the current 'truths' of the transformation effort • Looks for ways to evidence the leaps of faith made previously that have paid off in new knowledge and achievement of goals • Directs the bursts of energy released by people making a leap of faith

Chapter References:

5 stages of change described by psychologist James O. Prochaska 1977

5 stages of grief and loss by psychologist Elisabeth Kubler-Ross 1969

Synchronously Co-Create The Future |

Previous chapters have mentioned co-creation as a staple activity in bringing about a New Millennium mindset, a Millennials engagement mechanism and a critical tool in manifesting transformation.

This chapter takes a deeper look at synchronously Co-Creating the future and how co-creation feeds and fuels the efforts of interacting groups, teams, and functions in bringing radical change into realization over and over again without the fatigue, without the strife that many transformational efforts elicit and experience.

WHATS SO DIFFERENT ABOUT CO-CREATION?

Many readers will harken back to a time when joint design sessions were the norm for engaging subject matter experts and leaders in creating the future state. What's different about co-creation is that it is neither top-down nor bottom-up. It's from the centre outward and is an exercise of creating from scratch rather than taking the old and remaking it into something new.

Co-Creation is a creative process and recognized as such when it is introduced and staffed. Co-Creation has a broader mandate than joint design, whereby the objective is the right mix of ideas and solutions to generate transformation outcomes working with what is available and what the budget affords. Co-creation has little else to go on except the target characteristics of the transformation and seeks ideas and thoughts of others 'spherically' to qualify those ideas. As each solution is constructed from the ideas the Co-Creators collect the knowledge earned and tune the solutions so that they produce a more productive outcome and support the transformed state more closely. As projects progress the Co-Creators act in a parallel role to ensure the integrity and intention of the innovation associated with the solution is maintained and the Co-Creation process continues until the solution is implemented.

As compared with joint design, there is an absence of pressure with Co-Creation. Solutions are bubbled to the surface through dialogue and allowing of freedom of thought. The emphasis is to continually refine the innovative solutions as programs and projects progress rather than hand-off a solutions package and the associated knowledge at a designated time. When Co-Creators are stuck or at a point where a leap of faith is indicated, an injection of profound knowledge from outside the organization should be made.

Co-Creation offers part of a framework that holds the people doing the work together for the duration of the project or program resulting in a much greater pool of knowledge accumulation leading up to the point of emergence into operations and through that point into realization and the next succession of transformative change. Internal Co-Creation has a connection point to external co-creation efforts conducted with consumers (through social media, through market research programming). By aligning portfolios of programs and projects with the outcomes of external (consumer) Co-Creation - something traditional joint design practices don't do – a powerful connection is made between the staff of the organization and its consumers. See the section below for more discussion on this aspect.

CO-CREATION AND SUSTAINABILITY

Just like Uber transportation and composting, at its best Co-Creation within the organization takes up unused capacity and converts it into high value low cost products, services, tools, or processes.

The effect is two-fold:

1. Satisfies the Millennium need for valued contribution as a talent retention and attraction activity and an employee engagement activity
2. Brings to bear all minds to solving the problems and moving through the sea of unknowns associated with transformation

So, in a world fast becoming value-driven, the ability to apply and manage Co-Creation principles and practices has high – well – value. Not only does the Co-Creation practice go in the employee engagement, talent retention and attraction column, it is also fundamental to the principle of 'doing more with less'.

A dissonance associated with both consumer co-creation and the use of management consultants for the purposes of guiding transformation is felt when the organization seeks the advice of outsiders and takes that advise more seriously than the wisdom and ideas of own people's. Expect this dissonance to be felt as a disincentive of greater and greater proportions with the integration of more and more Millennium generation personnel.

Co-Creation offers a meeting place of minds, internal with internal and internal with external. However, in order for this to work, mindset that Co-Creation work is normal and fully supported must be present across the organization. In particular, the tendency respond to 'outside-of-the box' with dissent or condemnation must be quashed.

CONNECTING (OR SHOULD I SAY ALIGNING) THE DOTS

As we consider the importance of strategic alignment it becomes clear that all angles of 'strategy' need to be observed for transformational work. That is, transformational strategy has more dimensions than regular growth or regular (incremental) change and these dimensions must find alignment with the programs and initiatives that support their achievement.

In the case of co-creation, there are horizontal and vertical alignments to observe and track. There are also internal to external alignments to observe.

For example, when an organization takes in advice from its consumers through external Co-Creation activities or measuring trends in their opinion, it should distil them into the consumers' objectives for the organization and considered alongside, rather than embedded in, corporate strategic objectives. In this way, the consumers' voice is heard more accurately and taken in the right context when Co-Creation of solutions is undertaken internally. This can be thought of as synchronous Co-Creation with the consumer – a horizontal strategic alignment.

Similarly, transformation trajectories taken by the board and executive in response to transformative events must be defined as transformation 'identifiers' separate from the strategic objectives, which initiatives and programs align to, and measure the achievement of, as work proceeds. This is a vertical strategic alignment.

In the absence of a body of 'knowns', a greater emphasis is placed on strategic objectives in guiding transformation. By categorizing strategic objectives on a more granular level according to the source of the objective and its orientation and context, an envelope is produced for leaders and co-creation teams to use as guidance for their work.

Alignments should be made according to (but not limited by) the following:

- Traditionally expressed strategic objectives that support the strategic plan which in turn activate the realization of the transformation vision (employee engagement, consumer engagement, community investment, profit and loss/efficiency)
- Distinct transformational value 'identifiers' that are pillars of the transformational trajectory taken in response to transformation

event(s) that tag each initiative to signify its contribution to moving the organization along the new (transformation) trajectory.

- Distinct consumer advice objectives developed through external co-creation or opinion trending.
- Attributes distilled from employee thought capital generated from past initiatives, current and past Co-Creation activities, ingenuity and innovation programs etc.

These form a structure for internal co-creation work and the alignments between the co-creation of the transformed state through synchronous co-creation engines is a natural set of boundaries within which the knowledge worker decides how best to apply their abilities and contribute to success.

Understanding and applying a number of layers of strategic objectives can be complicated. Much more complicated than the annual business planning exercise and the annual capital planning exercise. However, in true New Millennium fashion, these nuanced objectives have greater importance than traditional strategic and tactical planning work during the time of continuous transformation. They create the pull needed to gain speed regardless of the volume of unknowns and as underpinning to motivating leaps of faith. A harbinger of success for the foreseeable future is the use of 'pull' techniques where 'push' techniques have been used in the past.

SYNCHRONOUS COMMUNICATION

The key and most difficult part of Co-Creation internally is the need for fully synchronous communication. Frankly it's a lot of work and most organizations are unable to sustain all the feedback channels necessary for the vertical feedback to occur that supports Co-Creation in particular.

A strong synchronous communication network that supports ongoing ingenuity and innovation among staff can take many forms. Of course the most natural form for this to take among Millennium generation people is internal social media, which is unfortunately the most un-natural form for Boomer generation people.

Managing the synchronous communication network and associated tools presents other problems. Like maintaining a broad but focussed thinking and dialogue so that it produces new ways forward toward transformation outcomes; avoiding getting bogged down in what is or isn't possible; a tendency to wish to avoid the breakdowns that must occur for transformation to be achieved; make sure all voices are heard without falling into analysis-paralysis or seeking a level a detail that thwarts freedom of thought.

This is heavy work and should be undertaken by people skilled in managing knowledge and thought capital. In fact the discipline of Co-Creation should be thought of as asset management of thought capital just as IT applications, manufacturing equipment, and intellectual property are managed as capital assets.

THOUGHT CAPITAL – THE MILLENNIUM's GREATEST ASSET

So now that you have your Co-Creation engine running smoothly, what do you do with all the innovative ideas and mental resources you have just stirred up?

First it is important to relate to your people that Co-Creation and the synchronous way of collaborating across the company is not a one-time thing. Stress that your talent acquisition and employee retention efforts are aimed at maintaining a constant flow of new ideas from among the personnel the company has hired and invested in.

This may seem obvious, but many organizations have a growing gap in employee loyalty and engagement triggered by downsizing, layoffs, and restructuring. Due to the Industrial Age separation, secrecy and control techniques, these activities were perceived as disincentives and positioned as either neutral/necessary or negative, especially as they were often combined with cuts in training and development budgets. As with most other aspects of business in the New Millennium a reversal of tone and approach is necessary such that it engages current staff in the work to reinvent, investing in them a share of the direction setting and supporting them with training and development dollars, mentors, and coaches to be able to succeed.

Not only does this approach present a more consistent and honest message, and a more equitable situation, it strikes at the heart of the reality of ongoing, continuous transformation. In setting the expectation of and equipping your people to apply more of their mental and emotional resources to the overall effort, both parties benefit regardless of whether this person or that person is still employed with the organization as changes are implemented. The organization wins greater application of the persons resources and the person wins skills and abilities that keep them relevant and in demand.

Furthermore, because Co-Creation and synchronous communication/collaboration put into broad circulation the wisdom and talents of staff, others consume that wisdom and talent and it remains with the organization until it is no longer applicable. That is to say, by creating genuinely appreciative models for working day to day, staff are naturally inclined to contribute the depth of what they know and are able to do as opposed to holding that back consciously or unconsciously.

The thought-power and commitment of people to the work of the organization are the most valuable resource the company has while transforming. Mobilizing and managing thought-capital as a corporate asset creates another 'pull' mechanism for moving transformative work forward with speed. The greater the harvesting and investment of thought-capital, the healthier the organization and the smoother (and cheaper) the transformation goes.

It is critical that meetings are productive and conversations yield ideas and actions without undue work in recording them by the people involved. Plugging synchronous communication and feedback mechanisms into Co-Creation meetings and also management and project meetings is challenging but necessary. New facilitative roles have cropped up in organizations that recognize the need to capture and translate thought-capital into innovation. These individuals have a depth of background in best practices and methodology related to governance and initiative management, they also have facilitative, coaching and change management skills to apply.

CREATING THE FUTURE AND NOT WORKING IN THE PAST

As the growth-by-projects movement has shown us, there is a painful friction between command and control financial management practices, and connect and co-create continuous transformation practices. This is one very obvious fault line created by the pressure of keeping one foot planted in each of the Industrial Age and the Information Age (not to mention a complete lack of acknowledgement of the emerging New Millennium 'Age'). Evidenced investment and demonstration of progress against ridged plans based on historical information can't support work that creates a new future. Basing transformation work in past contexts keeps the organization in the past.

What we will do can less often be predicated on what we have done as we move further into the 21st century. This is because a shift in sensibility accompanies the New Millennium, where brute force wins out less often than understanding and intellect. In fact, moving 'affirmatively' is the key to success. That is, basing the todays work on the emerging truths and knowns rather than past successes or failures pulls the work forward. Discerning next year's reality and working toward that rather than examining what did or didn't work last year is where the weight of effort should be spent.

Work as if you are already where you want to be, based on what is known at the moment and assuming what is known will evolve and become clearer – and that this will lead ever closer to the goal.

CHAPTER SUMMARY

Synchronously Co-Creating the Future Tenet - Central Concepts
- The wisdom, knowledge, and specific capabilities of each

individual are needed to continuously transform.

- Take up unused capacity and capability of the people in the organization at all levels in order to transform.
- The process of co-creation of organizational transformation carries the power to bring the transformation into effect.
- Complex alignment structures are needed to create the 'pull' necessary to navigate the sea of unknowns associated with transformation.

Characteristics of the Transformational Organization

- Fuelled by the unique combinations of minds in its business functions, groups and teams. Knows that at any moment in time, the right mix of knowledge, will, traits and innate abilities exist within the organization to craft the straightest and most optimal path to the transformed state. Knows that to contain the transformative effort to a few minds is to ensure it costs more and takes longer to achieve than is viable for the organization. Tends toward a think-tank mentality.

As it Appears In Communication	As it Appears In Leadership
• A transformative 'engine' will be assembled and reassembled over the life of the transformation to co-create the transformed state	• Leadership shifts in lockstep with the people who have the right strengths to bring the next piece of transformation into being
• What is needed from all staff is full participation in receiving advice and inquiries from the engine and supplying feedback into that engine as priority-one	• Leaders constantly stoke the synchronous feedback mechanisms horizontally and vertically across the organization is needed for co-creation to succeed
• Expect this 'synchronous' communication activity to take up a large percentage of your time	• Superimposing the more granular and specific strategic objectives matrix on collaboration and co-creation provides boundaries to focus innovation and ingenuity
• Recognizes the reality of the effects of continuous transformation on its labor pool and creates win-win scenarios	• Measures success according to the depth of synchronous communication, the participation that takes place and the regular completion of the communication loop

Enculturate the Language of Transformation |

Most organizations still speak in terms of Industrial Age methods and measures of success. In doing so, they unwittingly create a barrier to the mental shift at all levels required to be continuously transformational.

While technology industries provide us with a language for transformation and connection that is more and more pervasive in day to day dialogue, other disciplines can offer new words to describe what we mean when we talk to each other about our work as well.

Specifically, a tendency to still describe things in terms of controls and risk avoidance is deeply rooted in most organizations. While the CFO will take great offence and potentially offer great resistance to altering the expression of investment and throughput in terms that are nebulous and apparently random that is exactly what needs to occur.

This section identifies the lifecycle of transformation and some key shifts in wording and expression of effort that operate to shift the thinking of people as they approach their day on the job.

COMMON LANGUAGE

160

As transformation moves through organizations and continues over the next 30 years, a common terminology for referring to transformation activities should emerge. This book proposes that organizations enculturate the specific terminology related to the Transformational Organization Paradigm. Additionally, the time is right (the speed of radical change enables us) to unpack the box of pre-visioning work the organization must do to perceive a coming transformative event and so terminology related to the Continuous Transformation Management Framework™ is included here.

- Paradox
- Paradox Resolution
- Breakdown
- Emerge
- Sea of Unknowns
- Unacceptable Unknowns
- Acceptable Unknowns
- Leap of Faith
- Co-Creation
- Thought Capital
- Synchronous Ingenuity
- Synchronous Ingenuity Engine
- Transformational Value
- Transformation Lifecycle
- Transformative Event Trigger
- Transformation Trajectory – Implications – Vision
- Transformation Iterations : Construct Breakdown Construct
- Transformation Iterations : Emerge - Realize

The Millennium Age works in opposite ways to the Industrial Age. So reversing the thinking and approaches to work requires, and is accelerated by, reversing the language we use to dialogue about day to day work, projects, and tools. To achieve the greatest lift from pursuit of the Transformational Organization Paradigm, work to shift the terminology.

The values and motivations tables describing the polarized thought paradigms of the Industrial Age generations and the Millennium 'Age' generations point to the need for new terminology and language in the workplace.

Values Translation

POST-DEPRESSION BABY BOOMER	Y-GENERATION MILLENNIALS
Conformity and Sameness as Belonging	Diversity and Acceptance as Belonging
Mass Consumption Equals Wealth	Niche Customization Equals Wealth
Fear of Poverty and Loss	Trust in the Variety of Abundance
Milk Current Opportunities	Reach for New Opportunities
Follow Authority and Question with Care	Follow Value and Offer New Perspectives
Uphold the Status Quo	Disrupt the Status Quo

Motivation

POST-DEPRESSION BABY BOOMER	Y-GENERATION MILLENNIALS
Command and Control	Inform and Inspire
Separate People From Each Other	Connect People In New Ways
Separate People From Information	Stream Information Along Multiple Channels
Message Shortage and Competition	Message Valued Contribution and Experiential Learning
Give and Take	Share
What it Means to the Boss and the Company	What it Means to the Employee and Consumer

In particular, mental and verbal norms in how staff express themselves should be altered as follows:

- From Competition to Contribution
- From Control to Connectedness
- From Shortage to Sharing
- From Territorial to Transparent
- From Instructed to Directed
- From Self-Protect to Self-Express

162

- From Push Through to Pull Through
- From Denial to Acceptance
- From Faith in the Company to Faith in Self and Others
- From Fight For to Negotiate For
- From Exclusive to Inclusive
- From Doing to Being
- From Stepping Forward to Reaching Forward

In all likelihood the language of the new generations will pervade organizations as a natural occurrence over the coming decades. The point here, is that by advancing the shifts in attitude, a path is cleared for transformation to occur in a shorter timeframe and at less cost.

Afterword |

When I consider the messages from the Harvard Business Reviews 1990s I can assume that some organizations will have come farther than others in addressing the issues and concerns expressed in their pages. From my perspective, most organizations are still grappling with the key points in the reviews that resonate with the achievement or lack of achievement of transformation.

Looking at the past 30 years one can see that most organizations have been doing transformation albeit unaware. It's only since the turn of the Millennium that the buzz words Business Transformation have been coined, in large part in surrender to the recognition of the fact of the necessity for transformation. We have been trying to transform for 30 years and if acceptance is the hallmark of the beginning of real change, we have another 30 years to go.

If I could summarize the movements that organizations should make a priority in the next 30 years I would say...

1. A new way of managing programs and project or other initiatives is needed that centres on New Millennium principles and characteristics. This new way is exactly opposite to what has been standard practice in the past.

2. The organization must BE the New Millennium Paradigm to some degree before transformation can occur – optimally the expectation and mechanisms should be in place before spending money.

3. The New Millennium era is all about co-creation of the future over and over again – all hands on deck, all minds engaged to prepare the way for the Millennium generations.

4. Job-one is to eradicate 'punitive' seeming activities and responses across the organization and bend the minds of their people out of perceiving punishment as the intention behind the organizations demands.

5. The sooner you get to and move through the breakdowns the faster and more effectively you will transform.

6. Move forward only in the affirmative. Now is the time to be bold, move by faith and not by what can be seen, speaking only about what good has come of the efforts made to transform and about what new steps are shown to be important with each step forward.

7. Go for the learning experience, saying what has been tried and how that effort shed light on how the organization must act to renew and reinvent itself to meet radically shifting circumstances.

Above all, applying and adhering to a framework for transformation efforts is critical for success. Each leader must hold their ground in keeping the framework strong so that is envelops the work creating a bubble within which transformation can mature to a state where it can emerge into operation.

In practical terms, it is impossible to take on all the aspects of developing into a Transformational Organization Paradigm described in this book. Conversely, very little will be accomplished by developing only one aspect of the Transformational Organization Paradigm. Wherever you do begin, take on at least two complimentary aspects to gain ground in building the capability to continuously transform.

FIND YOUR EDGE AND STAY THERE

As a final word, I can summarize that the next 30 years will require an unprecedented level of courage and commitment in all areas of your organization – whatever the outcomes. A good deal of time will be spent at or near the 'edge', walking a fine line between success and failure, while neither success nor failure will be easily recognized. So, it is an understatement to say that seeking out the 'edge' and staying there is a critical success factor – the forward-looking viewpoints, the innovation and the efficiencies desired can be found out there, and half measures will ensure that your work to transform is a painful and wrenching experience.

Walking the talk at senior levels is essential of course. And seeing the work you do to transform through to its natural end is a birthing process, requiring as much surrender as strength.

Acknowledgements |

The author acknowledges the works of the professionals below in the inspiration of the concepts and practices depicted in this book.

BOOKS

Argyris, C. 1990
Overcoming Organizational Defenses – Facilitating organizational learning, Allyn and Bacon, Boston MA

Blake, C. 2008
The Art of Decisions: How to manage in an uncertain world, Prentice Hall, Harlow

Bowlby, J. 1980
Attachment and Loss Vol. 3, Basic Books, New York

Brown, J. and Isaacs, D. 2001
The World Café community, The Systems Thinker

Burns, T. and Stalker, G.M. 1961
The Management of Innovation, Tavistock, London

Bonfante, Larry eBook - 2011 Hoboken, N.J. - John Wiley & Sons
Technology Expert to Business Leader

Bridges, William 2003

Managing Transitions - Making the Most of Change . USA : Perseus Books Group

Crane, Thomas G. 2002
Using Transformational Coaching to Create A High-performance Culture San Diego - FTA Press

Clazala, Laurie and Walk the Talk 2006
180 Ways to Deal Effectively with Change. USA : Walk the Talk

Chodron, P. 2001
The places that Scare You: A guide to fearlessness in difficult times, Shambala, Boston MA

Chander, W. and Eisold, K. 2003
Psychoanalytic perspectives on organizational consulting: Transference and counter-transference, Human Relations

Egan, G. 1994
Working the Shadow Side: A guide to positive behind-the-scenes management, Jossey Bass Wiley, San Francisco, CA

Eslambolchi, Hossein eBook - 2006 Summit
Business Transformation through Technology Innovation, N.J. - Silicon Press

Evans, P. and Chowdhury, S. 2000
Management 21st Century: Someday we`ll all manage this way, FT Prentice Hall, London

Gerhard, Jane F 2001
Desiring Revolution, Second-wave Feminism and the Rewriting of American Sexual Thought, 1920 to 1982. New York : Columbia University Press

Goleman, D. 2008
A Conversation Between The Dalai Lama and Paul Ekman, PhD. Emotional Awareness - Overcoming the Obstacles to Psychological Balance and Compassion. New York : Times Books

Goleman, D 1998
Working with Emotional Intelligence, Bloomsbury, London

Hayles, N. Katherine 1990
Chaos Bound, Orderly Disorder in Contemporary Literature and Science, Cornell University Press, Ithica and London

Herrero, L. 2008
Viral Change: The Alternative to slow, painful and unsuccessful
management of change in organizations, meetingminds, Dubai

Judge, William Q.eBook - 2011
The Strategic Leader's New Mandate; New York, N.Y. - Business Expert
Press

Kegan, Lahey 2001
How the Way We Talk Can Change the Way We Work – Seven Languages
for Transformation

Kegan, Lahey 2009
Immunity to Change. How to Overcome TI and Unlock the Potential in
Yourself and your Organization

Kubler, Ross E. 1969
On Death and Dying, Macmillan, New York

Kegan, Robert eBook - 2009
How to Overcome It and Unlock Potential in Yourself and your
Organization; Boston, Mass. - Harvard Business Press

Kurtzman, Joel eBook - 2010
How Great Leaders Get Organizations to Achieve the Extraordinary
San Francisco - Jossey-Bass

Kaufmann, G. 1989
The Psychology of Shame, Theory and treatment of shame-based syndromes,
Springer, NY

Leaf, C. 2008
Who Switched Off My Brain, Switch on Your Brain USA

Leaf, C. 2013
Switch On Your Brain, Baker Books, Grand Rapids MI

Lerner, Michael 1986
Surplus Powerlessness – The Psychodynamics of Everyday Life and the
Psychology of the Individual and Social Transformation. New Jersey :
Humanities Press International

Lober, J. 1994
Paradoxes of Gender, Yale University Press, Yale University

Miles, M. 1998
Patriarchy and Accumulation on a World Scale, Zed Books Ltd, London

Morgan, Mark J. et al 2010
Executing Your Business Transformation – How to Engage Sweeping
Change without Killing Yourself or your Business;

Morgan, G. 2006
Images of organization, Sage Publications, Thousand Oaks, CA

Muller, Hunter eBook - 2011 Hoboken, N.J. - John Wiley & Sons
Leadership and Innovation Strategies for IT Executives in A Rapidly
Changing World

McGregor, D. 1966
The Human Side of Enterprise, Massachusetts Institute of Technology, MIT
Press Cambridge, MA:

Noer, D. 1993
Healing the Wounds: Overcoming the trauma of layoffs and revitalizing
downsized organizations, Jossey-Bass, San Francisco, CA
Sauer, C. and Yetton, P. W. 1997
Steps to the Future: Fresh thinking on the management of IT-based
organizational transformation, Jossey-Bass, San Francisco, CA

Sharmer, O. 2007
Theory U: Leading from the future as it emerges, Barrett-Koehler, San
Francisco, CA

Thompson, Lana 1999
The Wandering Womb, A Cultural History of Outrageous Beliefs about
Women
Amherst, NY - Prometheus Books

Fox, Robin (Book - 2011)
The Tribal Imagination, Civilization and the Savage Mind
Cambridge - Harvard University Press

Sanday, Peggy Reeves 1981
Female Power and Male Dominance, On the Origins of Sexual Inequality
Cambridge ; New York - Cambridge University Press

Ryan, M.J. 2009
AdaptAbility – How to Survive Change You Didn't Ask For. New York :
Broadway Books

Seddon, J. 2003
Freedom From Command and Control, Vanguard Education
Alsop, R. 2008

The Trophy Kids Grow Up: How the Millennial Generation is Shaking Up the Workplace, Jossey-Bass, CA

Various, 1998
Harvard Business Review on Change, Harvard School Press, Boston, MA

Various 1993 and 1994
Harvard Business Review - Harvard Business Press

ARTICLES

Acker, J. 1989
The Problem with Patriarchy, Sociology, Sage Publications Ltd.

Bowman, David
Are You Adept at Adapting?
http://www.ttgconsultants.com/articles/adapting.html

Brah, Aviar 2010
Difference, Diversity and Differentiation, International Review of Sociology

Baker, D. 1999
Move Over Baby Boomers, ABA Journal

Brunkhorst, Steve
Adapting to Change:- 5 Essential Life Skills
http://ezinearticles.com/?Adapting-to-Change:-5-Essential-Life-Skills&id=194914

Brown, Eric D.
Reasons for Resisting Change
http://ericbrown.com/reasons-for-resisting-change.htm

Chia, R. 1999
A 'Rhizomic' Model of Organizational Change and Transformation: Perspective from a Metaphysics of Change. British Journal of Management, 10: 209–227. doi: 10.1111/1467-8551.00128

Child, J., and McGrath, R. 2001
Organizations unfettered: organization form in an information-intensive economy, Academy of Management Journal

CIPD (accessed 2003) Organizing for Success in the 21st Century
www.cipd.org.uk

Dent, E. 1999
Complexity science, a worldview shift, Emergence: The Journal of
Complexity in Management and Organizations

Decision Guide
Resisting Change
http://decide-guide.com/resisting-change/

Dunphy, Dexter C. and Stace, Doug A. 1988
Transformational and Coercive Strategies for Planned Organizational
Change: Beyond the O.D. Model, , Australian Graduate School of
Management, University of New South Wales, Kensington, Australia

Eisenbach, Regina, Watson, Kathleen, and Pillai, Rajnandini, (1999)
"Transformational leadership in the context of organizational change",
Journal of Organizational Change Management, Vol. 12 Iss: 2, pp.80 – 89
Overview of Organization Behaviour in the New Millennium – author
unknown

Ferri-Reed, J. 2014
Millennializing the Workforce, The Journal for Quality Participation

Ferri-Reed, J. 2012
Three Ways Leaders Can Help Millennials Succeed, The Journal for Quality
Participation

Folbre, N 2009
Varieties of Patriarchal Capitalism, Social Politics, International Studies
Oxford University Press

Gill. Roger, Levine Niall, and Pitt, Douglas C. 1998
Leadership and Organizations for the New Millennium - Journal article by;
Journal of Leadership Studies, Vol. 5

Goman, Carol Kinsey, Ph.D.
The Effects Of Change On The Brain
http://www.sideroad.com/Leadership/change-effects-brain.html

Goman, Carol Kinsey, Ph.D.
Help Staff Deal with Change at Work
http://www.sideroad.com/Management/change_at_work.html

Gouveia, S.L 2008
Consumer Behavior of the Millennial Generation, Fernando Pessoa
University

Gallicano, T. D., Curtin, P., and Matthews, K. 2012
I Love What I Do, But... A Relationship Management Survey of Millennial
Generation Public Relations Agency Employees

Heathfield, Susan M.
Are You Ready for an Agile Future? An Agile Organization Embraces
Change; About Money online magazine
http://humanresources.about.com/od/careerdevelopment/a/agile_business.
htm

Hill, K.S 2004
Defy the Decades With Multi-Generational Teams, Nursing Management

Holbrook, M.B. 2000
The Millennial Consumer in the Tests of our Times: Experience and
Entertainment, Journal of Macromarketing

Kotter, John P. 1990
What Leaders Really Do, Harvard Business Review, Harvard School
Press, Boston MA

Kotter, John P. 1995
Why Transformation Efforts Fail, Harvard Business Review, Harvard
School Press, Boston MA

Kotter, John P. 1996
Leading Change, Harvard Business Review, Harvard School Press, Boston
MA

Kotter, John P. 2006
Transformation, Leadership Excellence

Klenke, K. 2001
Millennial Challenges in Management Education, Cybertechnology and
Leadership, Association of Management-International Association of
Management

McNeal, T.D. and Smith, R.L 2014
Communicating in Different Languages: Teaching Millennial and
Generation Y Students in Online Environments, DeVry University Journal
of Scholarly

Monoaco, M. and Martin, M. 2007

The Millennial Student: A New Generation of Learners, Athletic Training Education Journal

Montana, P.J 2008
Motivating Generation X and Y On the Job and Preparing Z, Fordham University

M-Y. Cheung-Judge, I. 2001
The self as an instrument – A cornerstone for the future of OD, OD Practitioner

Posner, B. Z. and Schmidt, W. H. 1994
Values congruence and differences between the interplay of personal and organizational value systems, Journal of Business Ethics

Prosci Benchmarking Report 2003, 2007
Best Practices in Change Management www.prosci.com

Raines, C. 2002
Managing Millennials, Connecting Generations: The Sourcebook

Robertson, C. 2005
Working with emergent change in organizations, Organizations and People

Smuts, B. 1995
The Evolutionary Origins of Patriarchy, University of Michigan

Sonnenwald, D.H and Pierce, L. G. 2000
Information behavior in dynamic group work contexts: interwoven situational awareness, dense social networks and contested collaboration in command and control, Information Processing and Management, Science Direct

Taylor, Matt and Gail (MG) 1938 to 2013
http://www.matttaylor.com/public/index.htm;
http://www.mgtaylor.com/mgtaylor/gg_origins.html
- Facilitating Complex Emergent Systems
- Future Views
- Creative Habits to Embed Processes
- Future by Design – Not Default
- Manifesto – The New Workplace
- Enterprise Restructuring
- Value Web
- Rate of Change

- Science and Art of Transition Management
- The Transformation Process
- UpsideDown Economics
- Group Genius

The works of Miller and Rollnick 1983 – 2009
–Motivational Interviewing
http://scholar.google.ca/scholar?q=motivational+interviewing+miller+and
+rollnick&hl=en&as_sdt=0&as_vis=1&oi=scholart&sa=X&ei=U8loVb7cKoX
8yQS95IGgCQ&sqi=2&ved=0CBoQgQMwAA

The works of Bernard M. Bass
– Transformational Leadership 1988 – 2009
http://scholar.google.ca/scholar?q=bernard+m+bass+transformational+lead
ership&btnG=&hl=en&as_sdt=0%2C5&as_vis=1

The works of Peter F. Drucker 1960 to 1995
- Innovation and Change
http://scholar.google.ca/scholar?hl=en&as_sdt=0,5&as_vis=1&q=peter+drucker
+change

Siebert, Albert
How to Develop Resiliency Strengths 1996 – 2005
http://resiliencycenter.com/how-to-develop-resiliency-strengths/

Thomspon, C. and Gregory, J. B. 2012
Managing Millennials: A Framework for Improving Attraction, Motivation
and Retention, The Psychologist-Manager Journal

Sweeney, R. 2006
Millennial Behaviors & Demographics, New Jersey Institute of Technology,
Newark NJ

Walby, S.
Theorising Patriarchy, BSA Sociology

Ward, S. and Chapman, C. 2003
Transforming project risk management into uncertainty management,
International Journal of Project Management

Westwood, R. 1997
Harmony and Patriarchy: The cultural basis for `paternalistic headship`
among the overseas Chinese

Publications in the Transformational Organization Paradigm™ Suite:

The Transformational Organization Paradigm – Thriving in Greyscale and Producing Results

The Transformational Organization Paradigm – Continuous Transformation Management Framework & Method PRIMER

Case Studies in Transformational Organization Paradigm Achievement

The Transformational Organization Paradigm Method and Continuous Transformation Management Framework Toolkit

Made in the USA
Columbia, SC
06 March 2018